The
Ben Franklin
Factor

Also by James C. Humes:

Instant Eloquence (1973)
Podium Humor (1975)
Rules Speakers Play (1976)
How to Get Invited to the White House (1977)
How to Be a Very Important Person (1980)
Speaker's Treasury of Anecdotes About Famous People (1980)
Primary (1980)
Churchill: Speaker of the Century (1980)
Talk Your Way to the Top (1982)
Standing Ovation (1988)
The Sir Winston Method (1991)

Editorial Adviser:

Time to Heal by Gerald Ford

James C. Humes

The
Ben Franklin
Factor

Selling One to One

QUILL
William Morrow
New York

Library of Congress Cataloging-in-Publication Data

Humes, James C.
    The Ben Franklin factor: selling one to one / by James C. Humes.
       p. cm.
    Includes bibliographical references and index.
    ISBN 0-688-14075-0
    1. Franklin, Benjamin, 1706-1790—Psychology. 2. Persuasion
(Psychology). 3. Franklin, Benjamin, 1706-1790—Philosophy.
    1. Title.
    E302.6 F8H92 1992   91-27581
    973.3'092—dc20   CIP

Printed in the United States of America

First Quill Edition

1 2 3 4 5 6 7 8 9 10

BOOK DESIGN BY LINDA DINGLER

To Mary

My daughter, who like Benjamin Franklin was awarded a degree from Harvard, and who would follow the steps of Franklin in reverse—leaving Philadelphia for Boston, where she became the managing editor of a paper—*The Harvard Crimson.*

Acknowledgments

First, I want to thank my agent, Bill Adler—who conceived this book idea and suggested the title. Like a modern-day Ben, Bill is a genius in public relations and book promotion.

I also want to thank my longtime friend Don Whitehead, who read the manuscript and offered suggestions.

As in all my other books, I thank my counselor, J. D. Williams, who is one of Washington's greatest persuaders. I again note my other Washington friends, Trevor Armbrister, William Schulz, Robert Smith, and Ray Tyrrell. Two of my oldest friends are former Congressman John LeBoutillier and Bob Butera, former Pennsylvania legislative leader.

I also appreciate the assistance of Jim Ring in Philadelphia, who was the first to see my one-man show, "What Happened at the Convention, Dr. Franklin?" My friend Eliot Curson in Philadelphia carries on the Franklin tradition with his skills in advertising and public relations.

I also want to mention those at the Free Library of

Philadelphia and fellow members of the Franklin Inn for their insights over the years, offered at the luncheon table.

As in my other books, Lourdes Monson was a faithful transcriber of my scribbled notes.

Contents

The
Ben Franklin
Factor

1

The Great Persuader

Captain John Paul Jones had a problem. He was a sailor without a ship. The American captain found himself stranded in the French port of Le Havre. Jones had come there in the hope of wrangling some ships from the king of France so that he could fight Britain in the Revolutionary War.

The captain had sent letter after letter from Le Havre to Louis XVI in Versailles, but no reply. He had made speeches asking for help. He even appeared at some rallies boosting the Colonial cause, but the only signal from the king was silence.

One day he received a package from Versailles. He opened it excitedly. But it was not from Louis XVI—it was from his old friend Benjamin Franklin, who had just wound up his diplomatic duties at the French court and was heading home to Philadelphia.

TO TALK ONE-ON-ONE CAN'T BE OUTDONE

Inside the package was a book—Franklin's own periodical, *Poor Richard's Almanack*. A flyleaf opened the book to a page. There, one of Poor Richard's sayings leapt out at him:

> Never try to ask by letter
> To talk yourself is far much better.

Captain Jones took Franklin's advice and went to the court at Versailles to see King Louis. He made his case and the king outfitted Jones with three frigates. Yet it was not in honor of King Louis but of Benjamin Franklin that Jones named his flagship *Le Bonhomme Richard*— "Poor Richard" in French. And it was on the bridge of *Le Bonhomme Richard* that Captain John Paul Jones, while fighting the British man-o'-war *Serapis*, would coin the most ringing watchword of the war: "I have not yet begun to fight."

Benjamin Franklin knew the powers of one-on-one persuasion. He developed them. He mastered them. Franklin was the first American success story. (In fact, he was the first to call himself an American!)

A poor boy, he became America's richest man in its richest colony. Though he had just two years of schooling, he would be given doctorates from Harvard and William and Mary in America, and then abroad from St. Andrews in Scotland and the Sorbonne in France.

He came from working-class parents but learned to charm kings. His looks were plain and homely, but he would make himself irresistible to the opposite sex, even when well over seventy.

He hated making speeches to groups, but one-on-one he knew the secrets of winning friends, convincing skeptics and disarming foes.

In Franklin's day the greatest orator in the British Empire was William Pitt, who was called the Great Commoner.

But Pitt couldn't convince King George III to keep him as minister. And so Britain would lose the American colonies.

In today's America, Ronald Reagan was known as the Great Communicator, but he couldn't persuade Speaker Tip O'Neill to support the Contras in Nicaragua. And so Reagan let his administration be dragged down in Irangate.

The Great Persuader

But Benjamin Franklin, who was no great shakes as a speaker, was the Great Persuader. In 1776, he persuaded a couple of Pennsylvania delegates to switch their vote in the Continental Congress. And so Pennsylvania, the biggest colony, led the other twelve in declaring their independence from Britain.

After Franklin signed the Declaration of Independence, he sailed from Pennsylvania to France, where he convinced the French king to back America and help finance the Continental Army.

When General Washington won at Yorktown, Franklin returned to France and persuaded the British negotiators at the Treaty of Paris conference not just to end hostilities but also to accept the thirteen new states as a full equal in the family of nations.

When he returned to Philadelphia, the Great Persuader had one last task to render for his country—at the Federal Constitutional Convention. At age eighty-one Franklin was too feeble to walk, much less to ride on a horse—he had to be carried in a sedan chair to and from the proceedings each day.

He was even too frail to stand and give a speech, yet still he managed to persuade enough liberals to buy the idea of a central executive, and enough conservatives to extend voting rights to the poor as well as the rich.

Finally, when the convention deadlocked on the issue of House or Senate, he broke the constitutional stalemate by persuading delegates to accept his two-house compromise.

If the venerable statesman was no longer spry, he was still successful in shaping a constitution that fit his own personal plan and prescription. And Franklin did it not by oration but by conversation.

He had fellow Philadelphia delegate James Wilson bring delegates by for a little chat at the nearby Indian Queen Inn or, sometimes, to his house on High Street (now Market Street). Then, with a twinkle in his eye, a chuckle in his belly and a timely saying on his tongue, Franklin lobbied for the charter he wanted—and got.

Beseeching Ben

By that time Franklin had perfected his powers of persuasion, which he began practicing at an early age. When he ran away from his family home in Boston at age fifteen, the penniless waif cajoled a ship captain into giving him sea passage to Philadelphia.

When he arrived in Philadelphia, he coaxed a man he met on the street to give him free lodging with his family until he could pay—even though the fellow had a lovely daughter around Ben's age.

As a young apprentice printer, the young Franklin hadn't the reputation to branch out on his own. So he talked the governor of Pennsylvania into buying him a sea ticket to London so he could study the latest, up-to-date printing methods.

When Franklin came back from London after three years, he found his old girlfriend Deborah Read cool at first. After all, he had left the landlord's daughter in the lurch when he skedaddled off to London amid rumors of his fathering an illegitimate child. Yet Deborah not only agreed to marry Ben but also to raise his bastard son, William, as her own.

If Franklin was the Philadelphia printer with the newest processes for printing, he also had a lot of other new ideas that he brought back from London.

In chats with friends, Franklin talked them into forming the first civic club, the ancestor of Rotary and Kiwanis.

At this Junto Club he persuaded two members to pool their books with his. Others followed—and so America's first library was founded.

When a fellow club member had to rebuild his house, which had burned down, Franklin talked him and his next-door neighbor into pooling their fire liability with his own. When others joined, America's first mutual-insurance company was formed.

When Indians massed in the Susquehanna Valley and the French threatened in the Ohio Valley, to the west, it was Franklin who mobilized defenseless Pennsylvania with its first militia.

His way was to recruit volunteers to bring a musket to a meeting. Next he persuaded them to attend a monthly drill and then to pay a fine if they missed a meeting. The fines would later pay for a company cannon.

Franklin was also America's first champion fund-raiser. He raised money for libraries, hospitals and colleges. He knew who the fat cats were and how to make them part with their pounds—yet still keep them purring with satisfaction.

The rich proprietors who ran and controlled Philadelphia didn't like the growing clout of this take-charge Boston upstart. The richest, most powerful of them induced his fellow proprietors to blacklist the young printer and cut him out of city and colony contracts. Franklin then talked his influential enemy into exercising his influence to make him the postmaster general for all the English colonies.

Benjamin Franklin wore many hats: printer, editor, author, publisher, soldier, businessman, inventor, legislator, postmaster, diplomat, scientist, statesman, philosopher and philanthropist. But he was first, last and always a persuader. Conversation was his catalyst. Talking it over was his tactic. Selling himself to an audience of one was his secret of success.

POOR RICHARD'S PROVERBS

If you want to catch some of Franklin's advice, you can find it in the words of Richard Saunders, a homely comic fellow that Franklin invented to outstrip his competitors by spicing up the pages of his *Almanack*, his monthly guide for farmers and shopkeepers that featured predictions on the weather, newest methods for plowing and practical tips on carpentry.

This droll character Saunders—together with his pert wife, Bridget—who Franklin presented on his pages, came to be a figure of fun in the eighteenth century, like Dagwood Bumstead of the funny papers and Ralph Kramden of television's *The Honeymooners* were in the twentieth—except that most readers of Franklin's *Almanack* in Pennsylvania and other colonies thought Richard was a real person. Franklin fed the deception by having Saunders take potshots at printer Ben for being a dense sort of fellow:

> Ben beats his pate
> And fancies wit may come
> But it may come, there's nobody home.

So behind the character of this cantankerous busybody, Franklin would dispense his advice to readers—how to live and work, how to spend and save and how to sell their services—and themselves.

Franklin was a well of wisdom on convincing clients or calling on customers. The lore of Franklin are lessons—in persuading your boss or directing your staff, talking to friends or communicating with children. Today the sayings of Poor Richard may seem quaint, but a closer reading reveals them to be quintessential.

If you want to know how to persuade, study his proverbs.

If you yearn to be a leader, learn about his life.

2

The Object Lesson

At the Treaty of Paris conference, which concluded the Revolutionary War, Franklin was a U.S. commissioner along with John Adams and Silas Deane. In the negotiations, Franklin was the key player, but the seventy-seven-year-old widower still found time to play in Paris—with the ladies!

Deane stood in wonder and Adams shook his head at Franklin in reproof. "Sir, an American who gives lease to his passions is done!" he said. Well, how *did* this septuagenarian manage to be sexy and win the ladies' hearts?

Even as a young man the short, stubby Franklin was no Adonis. Yet he attracted the ladies—and as he got older, he got better! He was described by a contemporary as one who "with equal ease could charm alike the lightnings and the ladies."

Although Franklin liked the ladies, he was no womanizer. Oh, sure, he had an earthy wit and a bawdy mind. At the Constitutional Convention it is said that in arguing against the president having a standing army, he quipped, "A standing army is like an erection. While it may enhance domestic harmony and conjugal relations, it also invites temptation for foreign adventures."

THE FIRST FEMINIST

Franklin's love of the ladies was rooted in healthy respect. The Philadelphia printer who was America's first inventor, first diplomat, first statesman, first economist and first philanthropist was also America's first feminist.

In fact, that was the main reason he ran away from Boston. His half brother James, the editor of the *New England Courant*, had been printing, as lead articles, letters from a Mistress Silence Dogood.

"Mistress Dogood" purported to be a widow who had taken over her former husband's business. She claimed that she did a better job of running the store than her late husband. Worse than that, she charged that women could be doctors, lawyers or preachers—and perhaps even better ones than men! Eyebrows were raised in Puritanical Boston. James Franklin was asked by the Bay Colony authorities to finger the identity of this Mistress Dogood.

James Franklin used to find the mysterious missives underneath the door of his printing shop when he arrived each Monday morning for work. So he decided the next Monday to come around five o'clock, before dawn broke—and wait. That next Monday, when he saw the envelope being slid under the door, he quickly opened the door and, to his surprise, found his younger brother Ben! James was so angry that he fired his fifteen-year-old apprentice/brother. A little later Franklin ran away to Philadelphia.

Franklin was successful with women because he didn't treat them as objects but as people. Unlike a lot of other men in his day, he listened to women. He took their opinions seriously and was interested in their ideas—so they were interested in him! Franklin was a character—a unique individual—and every woman he met he treated as if she were a unique individual, too.

George Washington and Thomas Jefferson may have had the heroic stature and looks to evoke sighs of adoration. Certainly these noblest of gentlemen were courtly, gallant and chivalrous. They complimented the ladies on their gowns. They admired their hair styles. They praised their needlework and applauded their harpsichord recitals—but they did not ask them for their views on politics or philosophy.

What contribution could a woman offer on Parliament's Stamp Act? What did a woman know about the philosophical ideas on the right of rebellion? Women at that time had little education, and the few that did, such as Abigail Adams, were considered to be not so "feminine."

Maybe because Franklin had only a couple of years of schooling—less than a lot of women in those days—he didn't treat them as if they were stupid, as so many men did. He respected women not because he wanted a woman's viewpoint but because he respected the views of any thinking person—male or female.

The women he met must have also liked the fact that Franklin was really interested in what they *did*. Franklin was unusual in that he did not look down upon what was, in those days, considered women's work.

The typical eighteenth-century gentleman would remove himself from the table after dinner to drink some port and take some snuff with the other men. Then he might talk about the new horse he had bought, the whist hand that had won a potful or maybe the pheasant he had bagged the past weekend, but Franklin could chat with the women of the house about music, cooking and flowers.

After all, Franklin, who was a composer of songs and ballads, invented the musical instrument called the armonica. You may know that he invented the Franklin stove, but did you also know he designed for his wife a unique larder pantry that would keep vegetables fresh? Did you know that he also built her a solarium in their home for the growing of kitchen herbs as well as flowers?

Don't Treat a Prospect as an Object

You ask, what does Franklin's way with women have to do with selling a customer or convincing a client? Everything! Customers, like women, know when they are being treated as objects—things to be exploited for profit or pleasure.

When I was a state legislator, in my twenties, I was often buttonholed by a lot of people who wanted a piece of me—my promise of a state job, my pledge to back a pet road project, my word on a certain vote.

And I learned to put up a defense that was long on good fellowship and short on specific commitments. In doing so I learned to appreciate the way in which women have to put up with men who try to put a suggestive edge on the simplest conversational chatter.

I remember a woman in my office years ago. A guy asked her about her vacation plans, and when she answered that she was thinking about going to the shore, the guy, with a hint of a leer, said, "Boy, I bet you'd look great in a bathing suit." People resent being treated as objects.

The lobbyists who were most successful in Harrisburg never confronted you with their associations' problems in the first few months. Sure, they took you out for a few dinners, but when they did they asked you about things that interested *you*, not them.

A former U. S. senator from Massachusetts once told me about an appropriation he was pushing for a town art center. The senator said that the woman behind the project always made it a point to meet him when he was coming to her city. She'd meet him at the airport, drive him to his talk, and during the ride she'd brief him on items of local interest—a winning high school basketball team, a local young woman now appearing in her first Hollywood film, the recent death of the mayor's wife. Only later in the many drives to and from the airport was the senator to learn of her interest in a local art center.

By helping to make the senator look good, she showed she was really interested in his future and his career. And so a couple of years later he pushed forward the project she was interested in.

Look, you can tell the difference between interest that is *superficial* and that which is *sincere*. You know the difference between feeling *used* and when someone is really *enthused*—about you, your family and your work.

Sometimes I think that the punishment for a brusque businessman ought to be to ship him off to the Tokyo office for a month. There he would learn, after some dealing with the Japanese, how he better take the time to learn about his clients—about their families and even about their golf games.

For the Japanese it is more than bad manners—it's *bad business*—not to develop some personal ties with a possible client or customer.

A woman once complained to me about her men friends. "Jamie," she said, "when you're talking to another woman you might mention things that are on your mind— you know, like you're considering changing your job or that you're worried about your mother's operation.

"Four weeks later, when you meet her on the street, the first thing she says is, 'Did you take the job?' or 'How's your mother?'

"But the guy from out of town that I was sort of interested in—we had a good long talk at dinner and three weeks later he calls on the phone and says: 'I just got in from Pittsburgh—what about going out to dinner?' At the restaurant he goes on to talk about his tough day—and the problems in *his* job, with *his* boss.

"But never in our phone conversation does he bother to ask me about *my* job or *my* mother or about any of the things we had talked about before.

"Men just don't seem to pick up on where you emotionally left off."

Being "Sensitive" Sells

Someone who does pick up where the other emotionally left off is what women call "sensitive"—and Franklin was that sensitive man. And a *sensitive* man *sells* himself.

A cousin of my mother's once told me years ago of her husband. She said, "At the end of the day, if he would just think before he entered the front door of what was the last thing that was on my mind when he left in the morning— maybe it's that talk with Bobby about his grades or the stopped-up kitchen sink or possibly the invitation from his brother to drive over on the weekend ... If he'd just remember what was on my mind in the morning and bring it up on his own when he came home, I'd let him do anything!"

Being sensitive sells; Franklin proved it and he was the first American success story. So as you drive out to call on a customer or client, take a leaf out of the "Ben Book."

Think of what the client or customer talked about the last time you were together. Was he or she about to go to Europe on vacation? How about his son or daughter? How is he or she doing in college? And did he trade in his car, and what did he buy?

Then follow up on the question: "What city did you

like the best?" "What was the best vacation you ever had?" "What was the best car you ever drove?" "Hey, do you remember what your first year in college was like?"

Remember, we all think we've had some crazy or awful experiences that make us different—and in some way unique. We all like to be treated as interesting *subjects*, not *objects*—and so does everyone else!

3

Don't Talk At—Talk To

In 1774 Benjamin Franklin was brought before the "Cockpit" in London's Privy Council. The royal interrogation chamber was so nicknamed because defendants were sometimes "pecked" to death. Franklin was being set up as a scapegoat for the increasing unrest in the American colonies. Overturning boatloads of British cargo and harassment of tax officials were just two of the incidents that had rubbed royal nerves raw.

King George III's attorney general was a little rat-faced royal toady named Alexander Wedderburn. To cozy up to the throne, Wedderburn concocted charges against the colonies' representative, Benjamin Franklin. The trumped-up indictment against Franklin ranged all the way from inciting revolution to accepting bribes from Colonial merchants.

In the proceedings, Wedderburn ranted his rage against Franklin. Franklin, in his modest wig and brown jacket, just sat there hardly moving a muscle, with a quiet smile fixed on his face. You see, Franklin sensed that if he said just one word in his defense, Wedderburn would toss him in jail for contempt of court.

Finally an exasperated Wedderburn, after four hours

of besmirching Franklin's character and his family without getting a rise out of him said, "Franklin, you're less than a traitor. You're nothing but a cheat and common thief."

Franklin's expression did not change, but later, after he had escaped a contempt of court finding, he caught Wedderburn in the corridor and confronted him, saying, "Anyone who strikes at one who cannot strike back is less than a man—he's nothing but a bully and a coward. But when we do strike back, you will find the master you serve will be a lesser king, for the realm he rules will be a lesser empire!"

A decade later in Paris, when Franklin went to sign the treaty marking the victory over the British, he was chided by his fellow peace commissioner Silas Deane for the ragged old brown coat he was wearing.

Franklin winked, saying, "I just wanted that coat I wore at the Cockpit trial to have a little revenge."

PERSUASION IS POWER, BUT POWER IS NOT PERSUASION

You see in your office those who butter up the boss while bullying their secretaries. Franklin hated the type who bow and scrape before the boss and then browbeat subordinates who can't fight back.

All his life Franklin would remember the time as a boy when his half brother James threw him out of his newspaper office. James had said to Ben, "If you're going to be my apprentice, you should know that for the next four years, I own you." Franklin answered that he would not be a slave to anyone—not even his own brother.

In a way this foreshadowed his position in the War for Independence against Britain. Franklin would not have Americans be slaves—even to their mother country.

Franklin didn't believe in talking up to masters or talking down to menials. Whether dealing with monarchs or maids, merchants or menservants, he treated everyone as an equal. Franklin believed that you didn't put one face to a boss, another to staff.

And Franklin didn't use one voice to someone whose help he needed and another to someone who needed him.

And Franklin didn't talk one way to a man and another to a woman.

Franklin once said that he was a member of no class because he belonged to all classes. Franklin credited his printing trade for making him that way. As a printer, he'd say, "I work with my hands, so I'm working class." But as the owner of a shop, he'd add, "I'm a businessman, so I'm a member of the middle class." And as a writer, he'd continue, "I guess I might qualify as educated or upper class."

Perhaps because Franklin was a writer, he had a special disdain for intellectuals who put on airs. When he was lobbying in London for the colonies, he first paid visits to fellow writers, whose views might be more sympathetic to the American position. He met David Hume, the Scottish philosopher and writer of British history, who issued a ringing support of the colonies. But then he called on the eminent historian Edward Gibbon, who had just written *Decline and Fall of the Roman Empire*. Gibbon wouldn't receive him, saying, from the other side of the door, "I decline to associate with anyone who would dishonor my king." Franklin answered back, "That's a pity. I was going to offer you my help on the writing of a sequel—'Decline and Fall of the British Empire.'"

Franklin couldn't understand rudeness. He always kept his Philadelphia house and shop open to any caller—be he a lordly proprietor or a lowly peddler. He believed in treating everyone as worthy of respect.

Snobs Are Slobs

At the Constitutional Convention one of the biggest snobs was Gouverneur Morris (Franklin would always stress the French *neur* in pronouncing his first name). Morris had a mahogany wooden leg that he kept polished to a gloss and wore imported silks from France. The affected aristocrat made a point of telling other delegates that he was the only one who could call General Washington by his first name.

One day, as General Washington was riding up to Convention Hall to assume his duties as the presiding officer, Franklin said in the earshot of other delegates, "Morris, here comes your friend George."

Morris went out to the steps to greet the general with a hearty "Hello, George." Washington's response was a steely stare of his blue eyes.

Morris, a secret Tory, had been slow in siding with the patriot cause in the war. Weeks later, at the convention, Morris would argue against allowing the poor to vote. Pounding his wooden leg on the desk, he had said, "There's no use giving the vote to the poor; they'd only sell it to the rich."

Franklin, who remembered Morris's conduct in the war, supposedly said, "Well, Morris, it wasn't the poor who gave these fancy balls for the redcoat officers, was it? And if it weren't for the poor we wouldn't be here today."

Maybe Franklin was thinking of such pompous bores as the magisterial Morris when he had the comic character of Poor Richard say, "Even he who sits on the highest throne sits on his own arse."

The Pompous Don't Persuade

Franklin had his fill of preachers' pieties, teachers' pedantries, lawyers' pettifoggeries and politicians' platitudes. Franklin knew that the real professional doesn't hide behind pompous language.

Franklin was the first real nudist in America—only he called it "air bathing." And similarly he didn't believe in covering up with a lot of fancy language. He used to scold attorneys at the time who would refer to their cases as their "advocacies."

And Franklin angered ministers when he suggested rewriting passages in the Bible so that the congregation could really understand when the pastor was reading the Scripture.

For example, this is the way he would have revised Job 1:10.

KING JAMES VERSION	FRANKLIN VERSION
Hast thou not made an hedge about his house and about all that he hath on every side? Thou hast blessed the work of his hands and the substance is increasing the land.	Have you not protected him and heaped your benefits upon him, till he has grown enormously rich?

Preachers hated his revision because, for one thing, they wanted language that only they could interpret—and not their Sunday listeners. That way parishioners would have to look up to them. Similarly, when lawyers, executives and consultants put up verbal facades, they're putting the rest of us down.

And that kind of puffery is patronizing.

And Franklin would needle politicians who would rather spout rhetoric than act.

Once when he was hosting Dr. Benjamin Rush and Thomas Jefferson, he asked them what was the oldest profession. Rush, a physician, said surely it was a doctor because the removal of a rib from Adam to make Eve was a surgical operation.

And then Jefferson, who had designed and built Monticello, said it was an architect—because form and order were created out of chaos.

And Franklin, with a twinkle, announced, "No, it's the politician. Who do you think created the chaos?"

Well, if congressmen obfuscate—so do consultants.

And haven't you also known bureaucrats and bosses who turn you off when they talk *down* to you?

That man or woman may have some expert training, but that doesn't mean he or she has to lecture you.

Maybe you think you don't talk down to people. But do you talk *above* people or *around* them? Too many executives think they can dazzle their clients or customers with the jargon of their work. Cant phrases like "our two-tiered marketing plan," "the multimedia positioning" or "the upscale-consumer profile" spew from their lips. These executives aren't talking straight to people. They are talking above or around them.

Have you ever noticed a television interview in which the commentator asks some union official about a possible strike, and the labor representative intones something like "We shall engage in a constructive dialogue...."?

Wouldn't you believe him more if he said, "We're going to sit down and talk...."?

Or how about the business executive who tells you, "We're still in the middle of some proactive discussions at the decision-making level"? Does that really reassure you?

WHEN YOU PATRONIZE, YOU DON'T PERSUADE

When you talk above or around people, you're talking *at* them, not *to* them. You don't convince people by condescension.

By the way, have you ever seen your children's eyes turn from you to the ceiling when you start pontificating? "When I was your age, I had a job...." "Sometimes I think you just don't appreciate how easy you have it—why, when I was ..."

If you want your children to listen to you, don't play Moses handing down stone tablets from the mountaintop!

Don't patronize your son or daughter. He or she may still be a child, but he or she still is a person. Remember, when your child starts looking *up* at the ceiling, you are talking *down* to him!

When you patronize, you don't persuade. Queen Victoria was once asked why Benjamin Disraeli had so much influence over her and William Gladstone so little. The queen answered: "Disraeli talks to me as a personal friend, but Gladstone speaks to me as if he were addressing a public meeting."

She might have said the same about Jimmy Carter if the Georgian had been her prime minister. Tip O'Neill once told a group of us, "President Carter liked to lecture more than listen." But Franklin would have won Victoria's approval and her acclaim as Disraeli did.

Franklin did not talk over people's heads or down to them—he talked *to* them.

4

The Franklin Formula

Franklin was a rare sage—a philosopher who wasn't preachy. Like Will Rogers, he served up folksy wisdom in the guise of a comic gent. But if Franklin didn't pontificate, he loved to puncture the egos of those who did.

Once some prominent clergymen quizzed Franklin on his deist beliefs. Did Franklin, they asked, believe in miracles? Franklin's answer was to take them, on a breezy day, in a boat ride across a pond. As the winds rippled the water, Franklin told the clerics he could calm it. With a slow shake of his cane, Franklin ordered the water to be still. Sure enough, the waves were calmed and his interrogators marveled at Franklin's power. But Franklin did not let on to the ministers that inside his cane was a tube of oil that, when he sprinkled it, could flatten the water's surface.

Franklin the printer could be a prankster, and as a prankster he often liked to play with words. In the 1750s, when he was the Colonial postmaster general, his frank carried the logo:

B. Franklin   *FREE*

When he returned from his years as representative in London to Philadelphia, the Continental Congress made him postmaster once again, but now he changed his logo to:

B. *FREE*   Franklin

When Franklin served as the colonies' representative in London, the king's prime minister, Lord Townshend, asked him to read over the proposed Stamp Act for his comments. Franklin did and told the British minister that it was fine—if he would make one little change. Townshend was surprised that Franklin seemed so agreeable and asked him what it was. Oh, said Franklin, just change the word *one* to *two*.

When Townshend reread the bill, he exploded: The only *one* in the bill was where it had said it would be operative in the year *one* thousand seven hundred and sixty four. The change made it *two* thousand seven hundred and sixty four. Franklin smiled. By his wit and wile the Stamp Act of 1764 was repealed.

Franklin's wit and wordplay reminds me of one of my own efforts as one of the White House speech writers in 1969. We had been asked in May to draft our suggestions for the plaque that would be left on the moon by the astronauts in July of that year. Playfully, I submitted a line that was readily rejected:

Just as Man Explores Space
Hope Unites Mankind, Exalting Science.*

The acronymic reading spelled my name! The scientist in Franklin, who discovered electricity in lightning and was

---

*The actual words on the moon plaque now read, "Here men from the planet Earth first set foot upon the moon in July, 1969. We came in peace for all mankind."

first to observe the Gulf Stream, might have disapproved of my antics, but perhaps the prankish printer in him would have laughed at my egregious ego trip to the moon.

And I also like to believe he wouldn't object to this acronym for his seven secrets of selling or persuading:

*T*iming
*A*ppreciation
*L*istening
*K*nowledge
*I*ntegrity
*N*eed
*G*iving

5

T-A-L-K-I-N-G
The Seven Steps in Selling

TIMING

When Benjamin Franklin came to Philadelphia as a young man in 1721, he found work as an apprentice printer. After a while he felt restless working for others. He was anxious to strike out on his own. Yet Franklin felt he had to have something extra going that would set him apart from other printers who were more experienced and better established.

Franklin had an idea, but it would mean talking to the Pennsylvania governor. Others who wanted favors might have asked for a royal appointment in the governor's chambers, but Franklin had no hope of that.

He had to catch the governor at some other time—and it had to be the right occasion.

Now, he knew that Governor Keith of Pennsylvania would stop to dine every Wednesday at four o'clock at a certain Philadelphia inn. So Franklin waited until dusk, when the stout satrap would no doubt be in his most expansive mood—when he would have finished his evening meal and be sipping a mug of fine Madeira wine.

Franklin, like Dr. Samuel Johnson, his English contemporary, reasoned that a well-fed man is a happy man. So he approached the governor's table just after he had eaten and said, "Your Excellency, you are governor of a realm that includes the second biggest city in the empire of King George I. As such you should have manifestos, proclamations and edicts with a printing style that befits such eminence."

The royal governor was bemused by the young man's suggestion and Franklin broached his idea. "Let me go to London and look over all the latest printing presses." The result was that the governor paid for Franklin's passage to London.

If time is of the essence, so is timing. You may have the *right message*, but make sure you pick the *right moment* to voice it.

Appreciation

As the first American minister to France, Benjamin Franklin had the job of asking for francs to finance Washington's Continental Army.

Franklin was a popular figure in the French court with everyone but Vergennes, the French finance minister, who would sign the check. Vergennes refused to see Franklin.

Franklin put himself in Vergennes's shoes. Vergennes considered himself a great intellectual, and he no doubt must have resented all the adoration showered on the American envoy. Here was this backwoods American, Vergennes must have said to himself, who was being lionized by the court at Versailles as a world philosopher—when he had only a couple of years of formal learning!

Franklin thought that any direct pressure on Vergennes would backfire, and he figured that maybe the best way to thaw his chill would be to make Vergennes do *him* a small favor. Now, he knew that Vergennes was very proud of his library and his status as an intellectual. So he wrote Vergennes to ask if he could borrow a book, a very erudite book.

Vergennes, who expected that Franklin's letter would be a request for money, was pleasantly surprised. In fact, he took quiet satisfaction in having a book that Franklin hadn't read. So Vergennes lent the book. A couple of weeks later Franklin returned the book with a thank-you note.

The ice between the two had been broken. Franklin's little letter helped open the door. He had sensed that any favor he would try to do for Vergennes would be greeted with suspicion, but that Vergennes would begin to like someone whom he had done a favor for.

Diplomacy is really public relations for a country, and Franklin was the father of public relations and advertising in America. With Vergennes, Franklin was only following his own advice, for in 1735 he had Poor Richard say:

> He that has done you a kindness will be more ready
> to do another than he whom yourself have obliged.

Some years later he had Poor Richard echo the same truth more cynically:

> Most people return small favors, acknowledge mid-
> dling ones and repay great ones with ingratitude.

Franklin knew Vergennes, after doing a small favor for him, would then begin to look kindly on Franklin. Franklin could appreciate why Vergennes might not like him because he put himself in Vergennes's shoes.

Appreciation means more than just appreciating another's fine qualities. It is appreciating their feelings and fears—it's knowing where they're coming from. In short, it is understanding their point of view. *Appreciation* is the ability to stand in another's shoes. When you appreciate, you approach a problem from the *other's* angle.

Listening

Franklin was the eighteenth-century version of a pop idol with the trendy elite of France. When he had packed for Paris, his daughter Sally looked at his plain clothes and supposedly said, "Father, you'll have to take better coats and breeches—the French will expect an ambassador to look refined." Franklin smiled and said, "I want to look more like a pioneer than a prince."

Franklin, who was a public relations genius, figured that by going wigless and wearing plain Colonial homespun, he'd stand out amid the bedazzling velvet elegance of the French elite.

The story is told of a ball that Minister Franklin attended in Versailles. Many of the lovely countesses and French ladies attending adorned their bosoms with Wedgwood cameo lockets of Franklin's image. While Franklin was with King Louis, one rather scrawny lady came up to purr over Franklin. When she left, the king commented, "It's a pity, Franklin, she does not do justice to her décolletage. God did not endow her."

"Yes," said Franklin, "but you, Sire, on the other hand, can endow us, for our government in Philadelphia, like the unfortunate lady in question, has the same problem—an uncovered deficit."

Franklin's keen ear and ready wit turned the king's

words into a pitch for the king's financing the Continental Army.

Poor Richard says, "When you speak, look in the person's eyes, but when he speaks, watch the listener's mouth."

Ben Franklin knew that often, our talking machine is turned up full while our listening machine is turned halfway off. We are so often concentrating on what we are going to say next that we do not listen with attention to each of the other person's words.

If you want to convince someone, you have to fully concentrate on what he or she is saying. Hang on the other's words and you'll hear something that supports your view. Listen for that phrase that helps sell your case.

KNOWLEDGE

At the Constitutional Convention, Benjamin Franklin, who was the oldest delegate, sought to befriend the youngest—Alexander Hamilton of New York.

Franklin had read some of Hamilton's essays and he had also talked with some of Hamilton's associates. So he discovered that the young lawyer was a worshipper of Washington, an Anglophile and even perhaps a closet monarchist.

Franklin shared Hamilton's belief in the need for a central government with a strong executive; he suggested to Hamilton that a president was an elected King by another name. He persuaded Hamilton that such a presidency was tailor-made for the majestic personage of Washington, who, because of his popularity, could have the lifetime tenure of a monarch anyway.

Four years later, just before his death, Benjamin Franklin received word from a mayor of a Massachusetts town. The town wished to rename itself after the Massachusetts native who had become the world's most revered statesman.

In their letter the town council had proclaimed its plan to erect a bell tower in Franklin's honor.

Franklin wrote back that he was honored by their decision to name their town after him. But he said he wished that the money that would be spent for the tower and the bell be used instead for the establishment of a library. Franklin added in a postscript, "I much prefer sense to sound."

Franklin, who set up the first library in America, believed that knowledge was power—persuasive power.

He had Poor Richard say, "The tongue talks at the head's cost." All of you know those who talk just to hear the sound of their own words without any real sense of the situation.

If you want someone to buy what you're selling, make sure you bone up on that person's beliefs and background.

INTEGRITY

When the Second Continental Congress completed its duties by act of declaring rebellion against King George III, Franklin told John Hancock, "If we don't hang together, most assuredly, we will all hang separately."

John Hancock, the president of the Congress, then pulled Franklin aside to say that the new government had need of his services. Franklin, with a laugh, begged off, saying he was too old to fight. Hancock replied that the Congress wanted to send him to France. Franklin reportedly laughed again and said, "A soldier has to die for his country, but a diplomat only has to lie for his country!" Franklin took the job, quipping, "I never seek, never refuse and never resign an office."

Despite his dig at diplomats, Franklin believed that you can't make others buy what you yourself don't really believe. To Franklin, any misrepresentation was a bad presentation. It was not only wrong—it was bad policy.

As the new minister to France, Franklin was supposed

to sell King Louis on backing the Americans. Yet the American Revolution was a rebellion against a king! The French king—in a monarchy that was already rotting from the inside—might be a bit nervous about helping America throw aside another king.

Franklin could have said he wasn't really against the monarchy in principle—only against the English monarchy—but right from the start he made his anti-king position clear.

In one of his first visits to the king, Franklin was invited to play chess. As the table was being set up, Franklin took the two king pieces off the board. To the startled monarch, Franklin flashed an impish smile and said, "In America we have no need for kings."

For Franklin, honesty was not only the best but the *only* policy. And you'd better be honest right from the start or others will soon stop believing you. If you are known for just feeding out a line, others will quickly get the line on you.

Franklin has Poor Richard say in 1736, "You may be too cunning for one, but not for all." Abraham Lincoln would improve on it: "You may fool all the people some of the time; you can even fool some of the people all of the time; but you can't fool all of the people all the time."

NEED

When the sixteen-year-old Benjamin Franklin stepped off the boat in Philadelphia Harbor in 1723, his prospects for success would have daunted a Horatio Alger. Imagine a dirty-faced kid in scruffy clothes. He hardly looked like a young man about to make his mark.

In his pockets Franklin had only three pennies, and when his nose picked up the scent of a nearby bakery, hunger forced him to spend them on three long puffy rolls that were almost the size of musket rifles. There was no way he could stuff them in his pockets, so he put one under each arm and walked off eating the third.

When he walked past a young woman she took one look at Franklin and stuck up her nose.

Later the homeless runaway buttonholed those he met to ask where he could stay. One man took sympathy on the lad, and the penniless Franklin talked him into giving him a room in his own house even though Franklin didn't have any job prospects. How did he do it? He looked at him and said, "I really need it."

Imagine his reaction when the next morning, he saw at the breakfast table the same young woman who had snubbed him—the same Deborah Read who would one day become his wife.

Franklin was not afraid to admit his need. Again and again he would raise money for hospitals and libraries with the simple words, "We need it—we need you."

GIVING

Perhaps Franklin's greatest service to his country was his last—when he helped to break the Constitutional Convention deadlock. Franklin saved the Constitution by giving in—by agreeing to include a Senate in the Constitution.

Franklin thought that political power should go to the many and not to the few. It seemed only fair to Franklin that the state with the largest population should naturally have the most weight. As a true democrat, Franklin believed that legislators should be elected on the basis of population—in other words, he believed in a House of Representatives.

Then the convention stalled in a fight between the big states, such as Pennsylvania, and the small ones, such as New Jersey. It was then that Franklin came up with the compromise—a House of Representatives by population, together with a Senate that elected two from every state.

To those who questioned the idea of having two legislative houses, Franklin made them chuckle with his tale about a man who had recently visited Washington's house, where the general was staying in Philadelphia. The visitor, when taking coffee, filled his saucer with it before pouring it into his cup. When the general asked him why, the visitor answered, "To cool off the coffee." And Washington replied, "That's why we need a Senate—the Senate is the saucer: It can cool off what the House cooks up!"

So by supporting the idea of a Senate, Franklin eased the fears of smaller states while meeting the demands of bigger states.

In supporting the compromise, Franklin spoke of carpentry: "When a board table is to be made and the edges of planks do not fit, the artist takes a little from both and makes a good joint."

In other words, if you want to be influential, look for ways to integrate others' ideas. Like the carpenter's joint, another idea could make yours even stronger. Sometimes when you give a little, you gain a lot.

If you try to insist on every little thing, you may lose everything.

If you learn to give a little, you'll get your own way.

6

Martini and Mellow
Timing

In 1940 Franklin Roosevelt was hearing reports that Joseph Kennedy, his ambassador to Britain, was talking about opposing him for his third term for the presidency. FDR did not try to call Kennedy on the phone to try to head off the Bostonian's maneuvering. Instead, he invited Kennedy to come to Washington for an overnight stay at the White House. Roosevelt didn't confront Kennedy when he first arrived; he waited until Kennedy had time to relax.

First there was a quiet dinner with a couple of celebrities that Kennedy knew from his Hollywood producing days. Later, the president and Kennedy went upstairs to the president's study, where Roosevelt mixed a shaker of martinis to oil the mood. After some insiders' Washington gossip about people they both knew, Roosevelt began sketching a political scenario of four years hence—in 1944, when the right presidential candidate for the Democratic Party would be one with a business background and who would also appeal to urban Catholics.

It was then that he proposed that Kennedy make a national radio address in favor of the current 1940 Roosevelt candidacy.

By waiting for the right moment, Roosevelt not only

talked Kennedy out of supporting Republican candidate
Wendell Willkie but also recruited him for a key role in FDR's
presidential campaign that broadened his Catholic support.

WINE AND DINE

Franklin Roosevelt, who was a fan of Benjamin Franklin, might have read Poor Richard's advice, "He that would
catch fish must venture the bait." Roosevelt had set the scene
for his cozy chat with Kennedy and had up his sleeve the
presidential nomination in 1944 to dangle before him.

In warming up Joe Kennedy, Roosevelt also heeded
Poor Richard's proverb on persuasion: "Never spare the parson's wine or baker's pudding."

There are occasions, though, when Franklin didn't pile
on the "parson's wine" or "baker's pudding." In the 1740s
the Philadelphia proprietors had banded together to deny
Franklin colony and city contracts. For a printer like Franklin,
whose shop depended on the printing jobs of writs and stat-
utes from the offices of the governor and the attorney general, such blacklisting was enough to run him out of business
and back to Boston.

Priming and Timing

Back in his shop Franklin printed up a finely engraved
invitation requesting the company of the leading proprietors
for supper at his house. Perhaps out of curiosity, eight of the
proprietors accepted the invitation.

On a bare table Franklin set out only one bowl at each
place setting. In the bowls was some dry, dust-colored mush.
With an earthen pitcher, Franklin poured water into his own

bowl, mixed it up and then wolfed the mishmash down with a spoon, smacking his lips happily.

The puzzled proprietors followed suit. But the first to swallow a spoonful said, "Good heavens, Franklin, what in the devil's name is this stuff?"

Franklin answered, "Plain sawdust and water. And you should know if I can live off this, you'll never drive me out of Philadelphia!"

The proprietors soon excused themselves and left.

Months later, after letting the message sink in, Franklin called on the leading proprietor. Franklin knew the job of Colonial postmaster general was open and he took the occasion to outline some of his ideas for postal reform. (As postmaster general he would institute a dead-letter office and pare the postal time for a letter from Philadelphia to Boston from six weeks to six days.)

The result of his conversation was the recommendation by the proprietors to London that Franklin be named the postmaster general of the colonies, who would supervise the service from Georgia to New Hampshire. The proprietors were only too happy to get this clever and enterprising fellow out on the road and out of their hair in Philadelphia.

Again, for Franklin, timing was his tactic for persuasion. As he had Poor Richard say in 1734, "He that can have patience can have what he will."

Yet too often we lack the patience to be persuaders—and the right timing for a talk.

A Time and Place for Face to Face

On one occasion when I was a houseguest, my host chose the dinner table as the place to confront his son on the bad report card he had just seen. The boy no sooner had sat down when his father demanded that he explain his poor grade in English. It didn't help matters that he did it with me present. If his father thought that by having a writer at the table he could better sell the need for studying English, he was mistaken. The boy was so embarrassed that he bolted from the table to his room.

At the time I wondered why my host didn't wait until he could be alone with his son. Mealtime is no time for confrontations. Wouldn't the father have done better if he had gone to the boy's room to see him in private?

There he could have looked at the boy's model planes or examined his baseball-card collection, and this would have been the time to bring the conversation around to what really interested his son. From there the father could have asked the boy why his high school English course wasn't turning him on. And then they could have both talked over what they could do to make it more fun and interesting.

When there's going to be a talk—*face to face*—make sure you pick the right *time* and *place*.

If you want advice to be constructive, construct the right atmosphere for that advice.

Choose the right moment, and you can turn argument into agreement.

On another occasion I saw bad timing wreck a possible raise. A colleague broached the subject to the boss right in the middle of a rush project, and the result was a curt brush-off.

Ben Franklin in that position would have asked the boss for an appointment at a later time, saying he needed some personal advice. No one turns down a request for advice. Everyone likes to be consulted and asked for their opinions and ideas.

If you're asking for a raise you could say, "Mr. Bigwig, you're someone I respect, and I'd like to know how you view the company's plans—its long-range future." It is an easy step from talking about the company's future to talking about your own.

At this "appointment for advice" you can ask your boss to discuss the long-range plans of the company and then shift the talk to your own role in these plans. You might even bring up some other jobs you're considering because of your expanding family commitments.

In this scenario you won't have to ask for a raise—the boss himself will suggest it!

Don't fool with your future by forcing the subject of a raise at the wrong time. Catch bosses when it is convenient for them!

DON'T OVERSELL THE SELL

But if persuasion is a matter of waiting for the right moment, sometimes you can wait too long. Top salesmen will tell you that the time to close is the first moment the customer indicates he's ready to buy.

John Foster Dulles, secretary of state in the Eisenhower administration, came to a Cabinet meeting with a fourteen-page brief outlining the case for foreign aid. About the time he had finished the first page, George Humphrey, the tight-fisted secretary of treasury, interrupted: "Foster, if this is about the foreign-aid appropriation, I am for it." Dulles stopped in the middle of a sentence. He had had years of practicing law before he joined the government, and he knew that once the other side has bought your case, it's time to stop talking. Otherwise you might say something that could change their mind.

A TIME TO HOLD, A TIME TO FOLD

And there's also a time when you realize you're never going to sell your proposal—even if you have all the time in the world.

Franklin, whose song lyrics suggest today's country music, would have agreed with the line from a popular ballad: That you have to know when to hold and when to fold.

In 1774, after the Cockpit ordeal, Franklin knew in his heart it was time to leave London. He had overstayed his welcome and he was anxious to see his beloved Debbie. In one of his letters home he wrote to her of his plans for remodeling their house (one sketch was for a double-storied inside john!).

But on the other side of the Atlantic, Franklin's fellow Americans begged him to stay on in London. Ten years earlier Franklin had talked Parliament into dropping the Stamp Act, but now he knew the time for talking was past. And he wrote just that to the leaders in Philadelphia.

Still, the Pennsylvanians pleaded. They said if they could just get their petition of a thousand names to King George, he'd understand. Franklin said of the Olive Branch petition, "It wouldn't be a hiccup in a hurricane." Franklin knew a storm was coming and it was time to leave before he got soaked.

Just as he was about finished packing, he got a letter from home. It was not from his wife, Debbie, but from his daughter, Sally. Debbie had died.

Franklin wept for waiting too long.

Against his better judgment he had stayed on in London—he knew in his mind the situation wouldn't get better but only worse.

As he thought of his Debbie and his delays in departing, he might have remembered what he had written as Poor Richard: "Lost time is never found again."

Franklin said: "There is a ripe time for persuading. Too soon and it's green and sticks to the vine—too late and it's of no rotten use."

7

Appreciation
The Peking Perspective

Long before Richard Nixon was elected president in 1968, he was contemplating an initiative to open relations with the People's Republic of China.

When Nixon became president, he consulted with old China hands from the State Department and top Asia specialists from universities to advise him on Communist China's reaction to such a move.

Virtually all the so-called experts told Nixon that such a diplomatic deal was impossible until the Vietnam conflict was resolved. But Nixon, who had traveled widely in Asia and had studied Chinese history, questioned their advice. He had come to the belief that in divining the thinking of diplomats, national interest is more important than ideology.

Nixon put himself in Mao's shoes. He sensed that the Communist leader might not be too happy about North Vietnam expanding its military might into Southeast Asia, with inroads into Laos and Cambodia. How would the United States react, Nixon thought, if Mexico were taking over the governments of Guatemala and El Salvador?

And Nixon reasoned further that the fact that Ho Chi Minh's armies were invading with the help of Russian money, equipment and military advisers would make the prospect of North Vietnamese domination of Southeast Asia even worse from the Chinese point of view.

Nixon knew that historically this Asian nation always feared and distrusted the giant "Caucasian" neighbor on its northern border.

So despite the fact that Communist China and North Vietnam were nominal allies, Nixon went ahead with his feelers for contact with Mao and Chou En-lai.

THE PERSUASIVE HAVE PERSPECTIVE

Nixon knew that persuasion was sometimes a matter of perspective. Because Nixon put himself in the other man's shoes, he knew how to present a case to the Red Chinese on opening relations. As Poor Richard said, "It's easy to see— harder to foresee."

Statesmen like Nixon and Franklin always game-planned the reactions of others. They plotted their moves by predicting the probable response.

When Franklin was postmaster general in the colonies, making his rounds in various cities from Charleston to Boston, he found that by the time he unsaddled at the local inn, it was evening and all the warm tables by the fire were taken. He could get only a cold one by the door.

One gambit he pulled off was rushing through the tavern door, bellowing, "A bucket of oysters—quick, some oysters for my horse!" As the perplexed innkeeper fetched some oysters, the other diners raced out to the stables to marvel at this strange equine that ate oysters. When they returned, they found Franklin snugly ensconced in a chair by the fire. "Franklin," they said, "your horse is not eating the oysters."

"Oh?" said Franklin, smiling. "In that case give the horse some hay and me the oysters."

As postmaster-general Franklin became known as the Colonial version of a company troubleshooter. When General Braddock was sent to the English colonies to direct the French and Indian War, he was told to call on Franklin if any problems developed. So when the farmers in Lancaster and York, Pennsylvania, wouldn't give Braddock the wagons he needed for his redcoat troops, the General sent an SOS to Franklin.

Franklin arrived at the Pennsylvania town of Chambersburg in 1755 to find General Braddock talking to a young Virginia colonel. His name was George Washington.

Braddock, his face as beet red as his tunic, stormed to Washington, "If these stupid German farmers won't lend me their wagons, by God, I have half a mind to take them by force."

Franklin then put himself in the shoes of both the general and the German farmers. He could understand Braddock's frustration at finding American colonists who wouldn't offer their wagons to fight the French invader. After all, if the French weren't driven back, they'd establish a stranglehold on western Pennsylvania.

Franklin also knew the beliefs of the Amish and Mennonite farmers—that they were pacifists opposed to *any* war. Yet he realized from his trading with them that their religion, though pacifist, had nothing against profit! They might not *lend* their wagons for a military purpose, but they would *lease* them.

And so Franklin cooked up a compromise in which the Germans would rent their wagons for fifteen shillings a day. As a result both the Germans and the general were happy. It was not the first or the last deal Franklin would swing for America, just by trying to appreciate each side's angle.

Stand in the Other's Shoes—or Lose!

In 1957 I was in Washington when Queen Elizabeth came to visit. From there she went to Williamsburg, where she attended services at the Bruton Parish Church. The ushers directed her to the Governor's pew, where the royal representative of the monarch was always seated. The queen startled her American hosts by asking where George Washington used to sit in the church. Then she said, "I want to sit where George Washington sat." That's what a persuader wants to do—look at the situation from the perspective of the other side.

A friend of mine in Philadelphia represents many baseball players. He told me, "Humes, I always think it out from the general manager's position. I try to think what he's going to say—that my guy's batting average has slipped, that my boy's injury last year could mean another bad one, particularly now that he's a year older, or that the team has another third baseman, a "can't-miss" prospect out of the farm system who won the batting championship in Double A last year. I put myself in his position so that I can position my client better."

When I was a legislator in Harrisburg, the top lobbyists never accosted me, saying, "Representative Humes, these are four reasons why you have to introduce this community-college bill." That kind of demand would put my back up!

The real pro among them said, "Jamie, I have some ideas that may be helpful in your Williamsport constituency." Then, over a cup of coffee, he'd invite my suggestions on a package that included a press release to all my local papers, a suggested photo opportunity of me guest lecturing at the community college and perhaps even a suggested fifteen-minute talk on such legislation before a Rotary or Kiwanis club.

The Rotary speech draft would include some local human-interest stories: the wheelchair-bound housewife who wrote a book with the help of the college outreach program, or the black father who went off welfare rolls to find work with the aid of the school's computer program.

The old pro would persuade me by putting himself in *my* position. He would study the legislation from *my* point of view. He'd talk about the matter from *my* political interest. He would say, "Now, Jamie, I'm not going to tell you how to vote, because you know your area better than anyone else. But let's go over some of the groups in there that could be really hot for this bill."

What could have been threats in the mouth of an amateur came out as some helpful advice. He made a "stick" look like another carrot.

A Blind Mind

Now, in 1919 if Woodrow Wilson had just tried to appreciate Senator Henry Cabot Lodge's position, he could have sold his plan for the League of Nations.

President Woodrow Wilson had returned from the Versailles Conference to champion his proposal for the League of Nations. Yet he never managed to persuade the United States Senate to ratify the Versailles treaty that included the plan for the league. Why? Because he never put himself in the shoes of his biggest enemy, Senator Henry Cabot Lodge.

Wilson knew that long before he himself first suggested some world association of governments, Lodge had been advocating, along with Theodore Roosevelt, a similar kind of international body.

If Wilson had not been too blind from pride, he might

have tried to look at it from Lodge's viewpoint, and then he would have brought Lodge in for consultation.

Wilson had to know that Lodge, like himself, was both a scholar and an intellectual. But Wilson might have been what Poor Richard had in mind when he said, "A learned blockhead is a greater blockhead than an ignorant one." Wilson should have let Lodge share some credit for the league idea. Remember how Benjamin Franklin handled Vergennes—another proud and prickly foe?

After all, Wilson was an author of books on government. He had to know that Lodge, as head of his party, had to deal with some of his party's reservations about such an international treaty. He had to realize that some of Lodge's fellow Republicans represented isolationist sentiments in the Midwest and conservative Irish constituencies in the East.

What if Wilson had met with Lodge and talked over how they could take care of these problems and then allowed Lodge to share some of the credit for shaping the treaty?

What if Wilson had tried to figure it from Lodge's standpoint? The answer is that Lodge would have probably sold the treaty to enough of his fellow Republicans to ensure its passage.

Look at how Harry Truman handled the same situation after World War II. To sell the United Nations, Truman made sure that Senator Arthur Vandenberg, the top Republican on the Foreign Relations Committee, was included in the planning. And so the United Nations easily won approval by a Republican Senate.

If Wilson could have called Benjamin Franklin in for advice, Franklin, that consummate negotiator, would have quoted what Poor Richard said in 1734: "Do good to thy friend to keep him, and to thy foe to gain him."

If you want someone to *accommodate* you, try to *appreciate* his problem.

Franklin, the man who invented bifocals, liked to say: "There is none so blind as those who will not see." Those who see things from only their own side are not only blind but bigoted.

If you want to persuade, look at the other's perspective.

"Appreciation" is to approach a problem from the other side's angle.

8

Listening
Grin and Bear It

President Dwight David Eisenhower is remembered as "the GI's general," with a grin as wide as Kansas. Lost in the legend is the actual story of the earnest military bureaucrat who was jumped in promotion over hundreds of others senior in service and rank to head the Allied command in Europe in World War II.

One secret to his rapid climb from lieutenant colonel to the presidency in little over eight years was that Ike was a listener, not a talker. The late John McCloy, who was formerly secretary of war, once told me that in the late 1930s Eisenhower ingratiated himself with three powerful men—Douglas MacArthur, George Marshall and Franklin Roosevelt. To each of them, Ike was *his* boy.

STOP, LOOK AND LISTEN!

Soldier Eisenhower knew more than just to stand at attention—he gave attention to listening.

Maybe he couldn't pump up the troops like Patton or mesmerize audiences like MacArthur, but it was Ike who made it to the top in politics.

A lady I know had the good fortune to sit next to MacArthur and Eisenhower at successive dinner parties in New York. She said, "Jamie, when I sat next to MacArthur I felt that at first I was sitting next to the greatest man in the world. But the next evening when I was with Eisenhower, I came away feeling what a charming dinner partner I must be—I guess it was the way Ike brought me out with his questions about all the countries I had traveled to and the differences I had found. He made me feel that my views were fascinating and that I was, too!"

As a military staff man for so many years Eisenhower had learned to listen—and listen close and hard. Along the way he developed the knack of seizing on others' words to serve his own ideas. That way he got others to voice *his* views. He got *his* way by letting *others* take the credit.

At a Cabinet meeting President Eisenhower might have said to his secretary of state, John Foster Dulles, "Foster, if I understand what you really mean about the reaction of the Soviets, it's that ..."

Or to Harold Stassen, his disarmament advisor: "Well, Harold, to boil it down, aren't you really saying ..."

They would agree and afterward President Eisenhower, personally or by note, would thank them for coming up with a first-rate solution. Yet his own agenda for the day would reveal that the solution was probably one he had already decided on. By his questions he'd *mold* other's views to *merge* into his own.

Even after he left the presidency he tended to lecture little and listen a lot. I remember one occasion in Gettysburg when a visiting business magnate offered some comment on world affairs that seemed to me to be about as insightful as "the sun will rise tomorrow." Yet General Eisenhower patiently asked the visitor to repeat it so that he could write it down. Then he added "Would you mind if I quoted you to Jock Whitney of the *Herald Tribune*?" who was then its publisher.

Listening Is Leadership!

Eisenhower's questions were tactical maneuvers—his listening, an art form of leadership.

As a military strategist Eisenhower was no MacArthur, but as a military diplomat he had no equal. He knew how to listen and ask the right questions. No one else could have persuaded such prickly and powerful personalities as Churchill, De Gaulle, Montgomery and Patton to all agree and hold to a common strategy and coordinated plan.

Another great listener who was a general as well as a president was George Washington. Eisenhower learned listening the hard way when he was a captain for so many years between the two world wars; Washington also had the skill of listening forced upon him.

At age twelve Washington had the height of a man, but when he talked there were still traces of a clumsy boy. In 1744 Washington, at six feet three and a half inches, was just about the tallest creature in Virginia. No wonder his widowed mother looked up to him as the head of the family. Why, at age eighteen, Washington looked so much like a leader, he was made the commander of the Virginia militia!

But if Colonel Washington was a bold soldier, he was not so brave about making social chitchat. Here was Washington, in command of many officers from the Tidewater gentry whose learning had been polished by tutors in drawing rooms. He could master a surveyor's map but not the syntax of a Latin sentence. Washington's knowledge came from the field—not from French instructors or fencing masters.

The president whom we remember as such an august presence felt awkward as a young man. Why, he even had to beg Sally Fairfax Washington, the young widow of his dead half brother Lawrence, to teach him the right way to hold a knife and fork and then, later, how to dance the minuet.

Although God gave Washington the stature, he worked to develop the style to match it. Then he let his appearance and actions—not his words—speak for him.

Franklin didn't yet know George Washington when he had Poor Richard say in 1749, "Big talkers are little doers." But a Washington was what the leader Franklin had in mind.

Inquire and Inspire

Washington would mask his shyness by making his speeches short. He found the less he spoke, the more people hung on to the little he did say. So it became his habit first to listen long, ask some questions and finally to offer his opinion—in one short, soft-spoken sentence.

In 1777 Washington listened long to "Mad" Anthony Wayne's battle plan to hold New York State, which he ended by saying, "General, I'll take the Hudson even if it means going through hell." Washington answered, "My dear Colonel Wayne, forget about hell, just tell me how you are going to take Stony Point."

When the Constitutional Convention opened in 1787, the delegates elected General Washington to chair the proceedings. His acceptance speech was one sentence long: "Let us raise a standard to which the wise and honest can repair."

Washington was echoing what Poor Richard said: "A good example is the best sermon."

That was always the Washington plan for persuading. At the convention, Washington listened and let others talk.

The only exception was during the debate about whether to put a cap of 2,500 on a standing army. Then he whispered, audibly, from the presiding chair, "If the army is limited to twenty-five hundred, shouldn't we have another amendment saying that no foreign nation should be allowed to invade America with an army of more than twenty-five hundred?"

In the first Cabinet, President Washington appointed strong personalities with widely different views, such as Jefferson, as secretary of state, and Hamilton, as secretary of the treasury. Washington used to cut off their harsh quarrels with soft questions.

He would listen hard to the pros and cons of a suggested policy and decide with a simple yes or no. Washington, like Franklin, persuaded not by exhortation but by example.

Washington knew that silence could be strength. He had learned that the best way to persuade is to listen, and the best way to listen is to ask the right questions.

Because his words were so few they were considered wise. Because he parceled them out they had more power. Because his words had more impact, he was more influential.

MADISON THE MANIPULATOR

If General Washington had a pet at the convention, it was "Jemmie" Madison, the diminutive Virginian whose notes constitute most of what we know about the convention. Like Eisenhower years later, Madison was the perfect staff man and became the favorite of three American legends: Washington, Franklin and Jefferson.

When the handsome Aaron Burr was courting the big and buxom Dolley Payne, Martha Washington took her aside and said, "The one you ought to be paying attention to is James Madison—he is the one who has the general's ear."

So when Dolly married the five-foot one-inch Madison,

some were surprised—but not the Washingtons. Madison may have looked like a puny clerk but he had a steel-trap mind.

It was said that Madison hoarded everything he heard. He persuaded by playing back other's views—but in his own words. He was the clerk who could sum up the ideas of others with his own spin to them. He was the staffer who steered discussion his way. It was Madison who would refine Franklin's words about the Senate "meddling with money matters" into the clause that "all bills for raising revenue shall originate in the House of Representatives."

Washington took a liking to the little Virginian whose words were often questions that recapped others' thoughts. After all, it was Washington's own style!

"SIX HONEST SERVING MEN"

As in Washington's case, my father died when I was young. But I remember what my father read to my two brothers and me before bedtime—one of his favorite authors, Rudyard Kipling.

Some of his verses my father drilled into me:

> I keep six honest serving men
> (They taught me all I knew);
> Their names are What and Why and When
> and How and Where and Who.

Try asking customers or clients these questions: *Who* are you now ordering from and *why*? *When* are you ordering and *why*? *How* are the deliveries now being made ... and *why*? *What's* your product being used for ... and *why*?

Franklin, who knew Voltaire, liked the Frenchman's advice, "Judge others not by their answers but by their questions."

Asking questions is the best way of listening—because questions show you really *are* listening. And by the way, don't be shy about interrupting an answer with another question. You're not really interrupting! You're only inviting the speaker to talk more about the company's particular setup or situation.

Then, when you have a clear picture in your head of the situation, make like Madison and recap in your own words *your* size-up of the situation: "Now, just to make sure that I understand your operation and some of the problems you're having ..." When you sum up his problems you're going to *seize* his interest—and *sell* him.

The customer will think—here is someone at last who really sees what we're trying to do and has some ideas on how to do it.

By listening, you set the stage for *your* selling: "Now, it seems to me that the cost is not a problem, but delivery is." Then you repeat his very words about late delivery. "As you yourself said, the shipping's a bit erratic...."

But keep in mind—don't in any way criticize his operation. You are dealing with a customer, not debating an opponent.

You are selling—not scoring points. Try to win an argument and you'll lose a sale.

Good listening is leading a discussion your way. It's framing the right questions to find the answer you're looking for.

The world is full of talkers and short of listeners. Talkers—even good talkers like Shakespeare's Falstaff—fail to persuade. Prince Hal told him what his problem was: "It is the disease of not listening, the malady of not marking that I am troubled withal."

If you don't hear what people really need, you'll never succeed in selling them.

9

Winston Woos Roosevelt

Knowledge

In the summer of 1941 Winston Churchill prepared for the most important journey of his life. He was sailing to meet Franklin Roosevelt on a ship off Newfoundland Bay. Churchill's speeches in the past year had steeled the resolve of the British people against the menace of Nazi Germany, but now he faced a different communication challenge.

A master of persuading audiences, he would now have to persuade an audience of one—the president of the United States. He had to convince the head of a neutral nation to give aid to a beleaguered Britain.

Before he left, Churchill virtually ransacked the library at the U. S. embassy in Grosvenor Square for information about Roosevelt. A former librarian with the United States Information Agency told me that Churchill's aides from 10 Downing Street scoured every file and shelf. They demanded every speech Roosevelt had ever delivered, every article he had ever written and every feature story written about the American president.

Churchill scanned a Roosevelt essay on sailing. He copied down the names of exotic countries in an article on Roosevelt's stamp collection. He read every magazine piece and newspaper column about Roosevelt, his habits, his family and his genealogy. Churchill discovered that they had a distant mutual ancestor, a fact that he tucked away for future reference. Churchill was trying to track down anything the two leaders might have in common—personal as well as political.

PREPARATION = PERSUASION

Churchill didn't put too much stock in the formal briefings by the British Foreign Office. He found out a lot of things the briefings hadn't told him. For one thing, Roosevelt, despite his Groton and Harvard background, was no Anglophile. In fact, he was suspicious of any British attempt to preserve its colonial holdings.

Churchill also sensed from his reading of FDR's speeches that the American president pictured himself like Woodrow Wilson—the world's custodian of the democratic ideal. Because of that Churchill wrote out their two nations' principles of freedom, which, on the U.S.S. *Augusta*, he invited Roosevelt to edit, rewrite and co-sponsor. This document would be known as the Atlantic Charter.

Churchill also realized from his research that FDR wouldn't buy the idea of direct aid to Britain, because the United States was still a neutral country. So it would have to be a loan. But loans to Britain in those dark days of the early 1940s, before America had entered the war, were a risky prospect. So Churchill offered the use of Bermuda as an Atlantic base for the U.S. Navy as a kind of collateral. The result was the historic Lend-Lease Plan.

Without his preparation, Churchill might never have persuaded Roosevelt to give those needed American destroyers. Churchill believed that you can't study too much about someone you want to sell.

The more you know about a future boss, a possible client, a potential donor, the better your prospects for persuasion.

What do you really know about the person's background, career, family and hobbies?

When Benjamin Franklin set sail for Le Havre in 1776 to begin his mission to sell the French on supporting the colonies, he spent his time on the boat polishing his French by reading all the writers currently in vogue with the court at Versailles. He pored over the contemporary rage, Rousseau, and caught up on Voltaire's latest writings and then he reread his thumbed copy of Montaigne.

Hit the Stacks for the Facts

Franklin, the father of the free library, believed that knowledge was power and that research meant results.

When you have that next big job interview—will you stop by a library first?

Library, you say! But where else are you going to read up on the company you're thinking of joining? If it's a national company, look up recent articles in *Fortune, Forbes* and *Business Week*. Then check out the index for *The Wall Street Journal* and the business section of *The New York Times*.

Remember, your interviewers have already read your résumé. They know something about you. What do you know about them?

Your résumé is now their tool. Let research be yours!

If you think that all you have to find out is the salary and benefits, you're gambling with your economic future.

What's the company's top-line product? Who are its biggest customers? How does the company rank with its competition? What's the biggest problem facing it? Is it high fuel costs? Japanese exports? Changing public tastes?

Look up library articles on other companies in the same business. Call people you know in related fields to get an idea of what's giving headaches to those who might hire you. It may be budgets, high turnover, supply shortages or top-heavy management. But whatever it is, it should color your answer to their questions.

Hit a Home Run by Doing Your Homework

In 1965, when I was about to be interviewed for a position as counsel for the Philadelphia Chamber of Commerce, I called my brother, who lived in Philadelphia, for help on how the chamber saw itself and its role in the business community. My brother gave me a few names to call, and from those people I got some information to help me in my interview.

One economist told me that Philadelphia, as an older Eastern city, was being overrun by service industries (insurance, medicine, real estate, etc.) and was losing its industrial base. Another executive gave me the news that the chamber was conducting a drive to bring in new companies from the outlying suburban counties.

So when I had my interview, I managed to bring up the fact that, as a state assemblyman, I had sponsored a bill encouraging the development of industrial parks—sites that would attract the manufacturing companies in land-rich suburban counties. That really scored in the interview! I hit a "home run"—because I had done my homework!

In the 1970s an acquaintance of mine interviewed for a speech-writing job with a major oil company. The job seeker had served as an intern at the White House and had, to his credit, drafted several sets of remarks that the president had delivered.

The twenty-one-year-old had hopes of landing a salary of $35,000, possibly even $40,000. His rock-bottom figure was $30,000.

My speech-writing friend made the worst mistake: He under-researched the oil company and so undersold himself! Sure, he was young with no business experience, but he had what the company wanted—at a time they really needed it.

Its profits were at an all-time high, but its image was low. It knew it had to beef up its speech-writing department and do it quickly. The speech samples the interviewers had asked for in advance—particularly some of the remarks my friend had prepared for the president to deliver to a business round table—had wowed them. But did they admit that to him? No—they talked about the bright future of their company. They were trying to sell *him*! My friend didn't have to sell himself!

They took him up the mountain and painted a rosy future in which someone with the right public relations skills might become a top executive. But when it came to money, they told him that $28,000 was the top figure they could come up with for someone his age, particularly since he had no experience.

The young speech-writer hadn't done his homework. He never learned that he was in a seller's market. He had underestimated his worth and the company's need for someone like him.

Francis Bacon said, "Knowledge is power." Everyone agrees but most fail to do anything about it. If my young speech-writing friend had gone to the library, he could have learned a lot about the oil company he was hoping to work for.

If he had checked out the business articles at the time, he would have read that major oil companies were trying to mask big profits by spending more in areas such as advertising and public relations.

Franklin had Poor Richard say, "Experience keeps a dear school but fools will learn in no other." My friend had a costly lesson.

CHECK IT OUT OR STRIKE OUT

I remember a case from when I was practicing law in upstate Pennsylvania in which a local farmer noticed his prize Holstein cow was missing from the field—through which ran the Pennsylvania Railroad. The farmer promptly went down and filed suit in the justice of the peace's office against the railroad for the value of his cow.

In due course the case came up for hearing before a justice of the peace in the backroom of a village general store. A slick young attorney had driven up from Philadelphia to defend the railroad. The first thing the Philadelphia lawyer did was to take the farmer over to the corner and begin talking to him about settling the case. Well, the young attorney talked and talked and finally twisted the old farmer's arm so that he reluctantly agreed to take half of what he was claiming the cow was worth.

After the farmer had signed the release and pocketed the check, the cocky lawyer couldn't resist gloating a bit, and he said, "You know, I hate to tell you this but I actually put one over on you this morning. I couldn't have won that case. The engineer was asleep and the fireman was in the caboose when the train went through your field that morning. I didn't have one witness to put on the stand!"

The old farmer smiled a bit and went on chewing his tobacco. Then he said, "Well, I tell you, young feller, I didn't want that case tried, either. You know, that durned cow came home this morning!"

Benjamin Franklin was the father of the American library. He knew the knack of applying knowledge to serve his own advantage.

In the matter of persuading, research was his reserve. The "Franklin Factor" is having all the facts.

When you want to be influential, dig up all the information first. When you want to convince, be conversant with the facts. What you don't know *will* kill you!

10

Integrity
The Cockran Counsel

In 1957 Adlai Stevenson came to London to address the American Bar Association, which was meeting there. The former Democratic Party presidential nominee met another speaker of even greater renown who was addressing the same convention—Winston Churchill.

Stevenson asked Churchill, "Sir Winston, what politician was the greatest influence on your life?" Churchill answered: "Bourke Cockran." The startled Stevenson—expecting to hear the name of someone like Lloyd George or perhaps Churchill's father, Lord Randolph—said, "Who was he?"

"Ah, Adlai," chortled Churchill. "You should know the name of the politician who, as keynoter in 1888, electrified the Democratic Party convention in a speech that opposed the renomination of President Grover Cleveland and, by the way, of his vice president—Adlai Stevenson, your grandfather."

Churchill told Stevenson that Cockran, a Democratic congressman from New York City, was a guiding personality in both his life and that of Franklin Roosevelt. It was Cockran who told FDR to get out of his polio bed and run for office, and it was he who gave Churchill a lesson in speaking.

For example, said Churchill, "When I first visited America in 1900, I met Cockran, a friend of my mother's, and he took me to a jury trial at which he was the defending lawyer. I was overwhelmed by his powers of persuasion, and I asked him his secret."

Cockran answered, "Sincerity—never speak what you don't believe."

IF YOU CAN'T CONVINCE YOURSELF, YOU'LL NEVER CONVINCE OTHERS

Shakespeare also said it when he wrote

This above all: to thine own self be true,
And it must follow, as the night the day,
Thou canst not then be false to any man.

The language of persuasion is the language of honesty. You can't convince others if you can't convince yourself. You'll never *persuade* others if you try to *evade* the truth yourself.

When Benjamin Franklin was in France, he didn't say America would beat England but rather that America would surely outlast England—*if* General Washington had the money to keep his Continental Army in the field.

Franklin knew that if you promise more than you can deliver, you are not only lying to your customer or client but also to yourself!

When you oversell, you only undermine your case. Don't try selling a proposal you don't really buy yourself.

In the Civil War Captain Samuel Du Pont was called in by Admiral David Farragut to outline his naval plan for taking Charleston Harbor. In explaining his strategy for blocking the

South Carolina port, Du Pont stressed the impregnability of coastal batteries, the narrowness of the harbor channel, the likelihood of Confederate mines.

Farragut listened carefully to Du Pont, and when the captain had finished, the admiral called off the proposed Du Pont naval raid.

When Du Pont asked why, Farragut replied, "Because, Samuel, you don't really believe in your heart you can do it."

In other words, don't try to convince others when you can't even convince yourself.

In the same war, a Confederate colonel with Stonewall Jackson outlined a strategy to capture a Union stronghold in northern Virginia. In his battle plan he kept saying, "I am afraid that ..." "I fear that ..." Sternly Jackson admonished him, saying, "Never take counsel of your own fears."

The Balance Sheet

Franklin had a formula for handling such anxieties. To a young man who was uncertain about an idea, he advised, "Take out a sheet of paper and draw a line down the middle of it, and then head it this way:

REASONS FOR:	REASONS AGAINST:
1.	1.
2.	2.
3.	3.
4.	
5.	

"When you do this, you find you will sell yourself. Then you can sell others."

If you want to convince others, satisfy your own fears first before you try to persuade others.

If you don't believe something yourself, you'll not only deceive others but yourself as well.

A friend of mine answered an ad for one of those do-it-yourself franchises that promise to put you at the top of a selling pyramid by recruiting others. When he called on me, I had some hard questions, and to one of them he said, "Well, I agree, that does sound a bit much but ..."

And I countered, "If you wince at some of their claims, how will you ever convince others? You'll show it in your eyes—you'll show it in your voice."

Three Half-Truths Equal a Lie

In the spring before I headed off to college, I called a young woman I had recently met for a date. She begged off, saying: "Jamie, I have this college application to do and then I think my girlfriend is coming over tonight and, anyway, Jamie, I think I have this awful cold coming on."

When I relayed her comments to my mother for her feminine assessment she said, "Jamie, you can forget about her. She doesn't want to see you now or next week. You don't really believe all those excuses, do you? She's not telling you the truth—three half excuses equal a lie, or at least a white lie."

"If the college application," my mother explained, "was really bothering her, that's all she'd have talked about, and she'd have invited you over to help her write it. If her girlfriend was really coming over, she'd have said, 'Gee, I'd like to but Susie called me in tears about a family argument and she's coming over just after dinner.' And if she really has a cold, you'd have heard it in her voice. . . ."

The fact was that she just plain didn't want to go out with me! Sure, she'd tried to sugarcoat her refusal with an excuse, and because she knew it was weak, added two more excuses for good measure. She didn't really believe in what she was saying and couldn't make me believe it, either.

As Franklin said, "Don't try to sell a half-truth, because it's often the biggest lie."

ENUMERATE REASONS AND ELIMINATE BELIEF

I lost one of the first cases I ever tried when the jury didn't believe my plea that the other driver was negligent.

I thought of my mother's advice of "three half excuses make a lie" when an old lawyer who had watched my presentation gave me this advice: "The young lawyer thinks that he can persuade by piling on a lot of reasons. You're defending, not debating. Pick the reason you really believe in and hammer away at that to the jury. When you're passionate about something, you persuade. Oh, sure, you can mention the other points, but pound away at the one you really believe in."

Then the old friend lawyer reminisced: "You know, once when I was defending a husband on a murder charge by arguing that it was accidental homicide, I said in my closing, 'Members of the jury, I could remind you that my client didn't like guns and had never handled one in his life, and that it was the gun of his wife's father, not his; I could mention again that there's never been a suggestion of violence in his life; I could remind you again that only a speed-car driver could have driven from Wilkes-Barre to Williamsport in an hour and a half and been there for the time of the shooting. But what I want to leave with you is that my client loved his wife—he adored her, he idolized her, worshipped her ...'

"And then I went over all the acts of tenderness and the notes of love he showered on her over the years—why, the women in the jury had tears in their eyes when I finished—and I got an acquittal.

"You see, I always believed that in a plea to a jury, you had to go with what you believed in the most."

PERSUASION IS PASSION

Persuasion is sometimes a matter of passion. When people see that you really care about something, you're convincing. Without integrity you'll never influence others.

Franklin once wrote down a list of virtues. Integrity, or sincerity, he stressed, was essential. He later wrote: "One must speak with integrity, honesty and sincerity."

Benjamin Franklin had Poor Richard say in 1736, "An empty bag does not stand upright."

What Franklin meant was that man without integrity cannot inspire others—that a man who isn't sincere cannot sell others.

11

Need
Bench Strength

Arthur Goldberg had the best job in America. He was a Supreme Court justice. Being on the Supreme Court was better than being president. Why, a justice, in many ways, was more powerful than the president—and he didn't have to face the voters. It was a lifetime appointment! Yet Arthur Goldberg would quit the Supreme Court in 1966 to become the ambassador to the United Nations.

How could a lawyer step down from the greatest lawyer's job on earth and take a job in the U. N. that had such little real power—in an organization that's been described as a "world debating society"? What did President Lyndon Johnson say to Goldberg to persuade him to leave the Court for the U. N.?

Once Goldberg sat down in the Oval Office, Johnson confided to him that the growing controversy of the Vietnam War demanded an American advocate of world renown and prestige who could argue our position to Third World nations. Johnson knew how to lay it on thick, but the bottom line came when the towering Johnson leaned over to Goldberg and, while straightening the justice's tie, drawled, "Arthur, the country needs you—your president needs you."

THE THREE POWER WORDS OF
PERSUASION: "I NEED YOU"

In 1776 Thomas Jefferson was also a reluctant re-cruit—he did not seek the job of drafting the Declaration of Independence. One might think that someone as young as the thirty-two-year-old Virginian would have greeted the job of writing such a momentous document as the chance of a lifetime.

But Jefferson knew that a young man's words were grist in the mill for men who were older and thought they were wiser. Jefferson didn't like the idea of Franklin and Adams, who also served on the Declaration committee, chopping up his carefully crafted words.

How did Franklin persuade the hesitant Jefferson? He said the magic words: "Tom, your country needs you."

After Winston Churchill delivered his Iron Curtain address, he was asked by an American reporter, "Mr. Churchill, what do you think was the greatest speech you ever delivered?"

Churchill thought for a moment and answered, "The greatest speech I ever delivered was in a gazebo to an audi-ence of one. In 1908 I was walking in the gardens of Blenheim Palace, hand in hand with a young woman named Clementine Hozier. A sudden storm erupted. We retreated to the shelter of the gazebo and there, with the rain pelting on the roof, I asked for her hand. It had to be my greatest speech because she accepted!"

Today we don't know his exact words, but we know how it must have ended: "Clemmie, I love you—I need you."

"Only You Can Make My Dreams Come True"

When I was in school in England, a sister of a friend was being rushed by an Anglo-Saxon version of a Greek god. Derek, this strapping blond Hercules, had won his "rugby Blue" at Oxford—where he had also won a "first" in foreign languages. Yet, to her mother's shock and chagrin, she married Percy, a Woody Allen clone.

I asked her whether she had heard from the dashing Derek—without mentioning Percy. "Oh, Jamie," she said, "you're like mother—you never understood why it's Percy and not Derek. You see, Derek didn't need me—but Percy did. To Percy, I was the only woman—I mean, the only woman in the world!"

Everyone likes to hear what Adam must have said to Eve: "You're the only woman I could ever love—in fact, Eve, you're the only woman in the world!"

In that tale of love there is a lesson—there's no more powerful feeling than to feel really *needed*, particularly when you're the only one who can fill that need. When someone makes you feel singular and extra special, you're a star!

John Ringling North, the young head of Ringling Bros., Barnum & Bailey Circus, once called upon the city editor of the *St. Louis Post-Dispatch*. At the editor's desk he said, "Hello, and happy tidings—the circus is in town!" The editor scowled and said, "What circus?"

North threw his hands in the air. "What circus? When they say the band is playing 'God Save the Queen' do you ask 'What queen?' "

Well, each of us feels unique by his or her own experiences.

Shakespeare had Hamlet say, "O God! I could be

bounded in a nutshell, and count myself a king of infinite space."

We hear a lot about the "common man." But none of us feels all that "common." Doesn't each of us think that we've had *uncommon* experiences, and *uncommon* encounters with life and death?

We may think that someone has led a sheltered, narrow life. You look at that man or woman opposite you on the bus or train and think what a humdrum existence he or she must lead—but do we know all the triumphs and tragedies in that person's past? Do we know all the successes and sadnesses that make that person's life so special?

When I wrote for President Ford, he honored in the Rose Garden a black school teacher from North Carolina. He asked her, "What grade do you teach?"

She politely but pointedly replied, "Mr. President, I teach children, not grades." She was a great teacher because she didn't think in terms of a "grade"—she saw each student as an individual.

We reject being stereotyped racially or religiously—Black, Jewish, Polish or WASP. And we don't like it when we're labeled politically or socially. *Yuppie, hippie, Archie Bunker*, are ugly terms. So are *bimbo, jock* and *women's libber*. To be categorized is to be cast aside. To be stereotyped is to be shrunken in self-worth. To be labeled is to lose identity.

And when a listener feels he or she is losing identity, he or she begins losing interest in what you are saying.

People may scoff at Dale Carnegie, but he had it right when he drilled salesmen to keep repeating the customer's name every two sentences. Our name is unique, and we respond to someone talking just to us, to our situation, to our problem, to our needs.

We are told that everyone's fingerprint is unique. Well, everyone's life etches its own imprint. The person whose career and background you might think is so stereotypical thinks of himself or herself as someone *special*.

TALK TO TALENTS, NOT TYPES

And we respond positively to a request when the asker takes notice of our special talents, our unusual qualities, our unique background.

I was recently asked to write an article to be published in a school magazine on the importance of the English language and the necessity to learn and speak it well. I hesitated; I wasn't going to be paid. I didn't go to the school and neither had any of my family. Yet I agreed. Why? Because the woman from the magazine said, "Mr. Humes, you are the only one in the world who has written biographies of the two greatest Englishmen—Churchill and Shakespeare." I couldn't refuse. My uniqueness was recognized!

It's hard for someone to say no when he or she is the only one who can fill a need.

Did Goldberg say no when LBJ said he was the only one who had both the eminence of high judicial office and the experience as a labor leader—and that no one else could better represent America to the struggling nations of the Third World?

Did Jefferson say no when Franklin said he was the only delegate who had read such philosophers as Locke and Hobbes and who also had already written resolves for the Virginia assembly?

If you want to *persuade*—be *personal*.

Ask yourself what talent makes this person unique, what in the person's background is special. Don't say, "I need help." Say, "I need *you!*"

You want someone to do a job? Perform a service? Help a cause?

Well, whatever you seek—think *unique*!

Remember that the last letter in persuasion is *n*—and it stands for *need*, that is, we *need* you.

12

Giving
Governor God

The first time I ever saw Jimmy Carter, he was still governor. At that time I already had left the Nixon White House and was practicing law while serving as a consultant to different federal agencies. One of these was the Appalachian Regional Commission. I met the Georgia governor at a commission meeting that he was chairing.

Governor Carter was unhappy with a change in policy that he felt worked against the interests of Georgia and in favor of Virginia, Tennessee and North Carolina. Certainly the governor was entitled to his judgment, and he might have been right as far as Georgia was concerned. But what I will never forget are his words to me after we had tried to explain the new policy: "Jimmy—I can call you Jimmy, can't I? That's what they call me.... Now, Jimmy, when I go to bed tonight, I am going to get on my knees and pray that God, in his infinite wisdom, opens your eyes to the injustice the administration is perpetrating on the people of Georgia...."

That kind of narrow-mindedness doesn't help the path of negotiation. To be fair, Carter had his triumph at his Camp David summit with Israel and Egypt. But President Carter was not as successful in dealing with Congress, even though his party controlled it. Dogmatism was his difficulty. And such intransigence other politicians find insufferable!

PRAGMATISM, YES; DOGMATISM, NO!

In 1951 Prime Minister Winston Churchill flew to Cyprus with his defense minister, Harold Macmillan. On the plane Churchill asked Macmillan, "Harold, what kind of fellow is this Archbishop Makarios? Is this new leader of Cyprus one of those priestly, ascetic men of the cloth concerned with the rewards of the spiritual hereafter, or is he one of those crafty, scheming prelates concerned, rather, with temporal gain?"

Macmillan replied, "Regrettably, Prime Minister, he seems to be one of the latter."

"Good," said Churchill, clapping his hands together. "He is one of our kind and I can work with him!"

Churchill disliked dealing with the righteous. He said of Woodrow Wilson at Versailles, "Moses had only ten points but Wilson had fourteen!" Churchill wrote later of Wilson, "There is no greater folly than intolerant idealism."

The righteousness of Wilson reminds one of the theological argument an Anglican bishop had with the Catholic Cardinal Henley. After heated words, the Anglican cleric said, "We shouldn't argue, Cardinal—after all, we both do the work of the Lord."

"Yes," replied Cardinal Henley, "you in your way and I in *His*."

Franklin said the same thing jokingly: "Orthodoxy is my 'doxy,' but your 'doxy' is heterodoxy."

Once Franklin was approached by a leader of the Dunkard Church, an offshoot of the Mennonites. The pastor said it was losing membership, and he wanted Franklin's advice.

Franklin, a printer, said that perhaps the church should publish and circulate its doctrines.

"Oh, no," said the pastor, "we have no doctrines written down because we don't know when another of God's spiritual truths will be revealed."

Franklin marveled at a religion that was so open to new revelations—that would give way to a new truth and not see it as a threat to its own existence.

To Be Headstrong Is to Be Head-Wrong

When Franklin was in Paris, he witnessed the first flight of a man-carrying balloon. Much money had been spent on the experiment.

Most of Paris scoffed. One Parisian said to Franklin, "What good is it?" Franklin answered, "What good is a newborn baby? It is a child. Perhaps it won't amount to much. Perhaps it will be very brilliant. We have to wait and see its education first."

For the inventor Franklin, some new idea just might be the kernel of something bigger, an idea might be an instrument for the betterment of mankind.

Franklin never closed his mind to another viewpoint. When the other side raised a question or suggested a change, he wouldn't dismiss it outright. To Franklin, to be headstrong was to be head-wrong.

As a leader of the biggest delegation to the Constitutional Convention, Franklin could have continued to insist on only one legislative house based on population—even if it broke up the convention. (After all, under the old Articles of Confederation, which he helped frame, Pennsylvania would continue to be the most powerful state.) Instead, Franklin listened patiently to the small states' arguments to see if there was some way their ideas could be incorporated. The result was his two-house compromise.

Many years earlier, as a legislator for the colony of Pennsylvania, he had introduced an appropriation to pay for the building of a Philadelphia hospital. The opponents of the bill had heatedly charged that if such a bill were enacted, people soon wouldn't be giving any money to charities— that private donations would dry up. Franklin had answered their argument with an amendment.

What Franklin proposed—the idea of "matched giving"—would revolutionize fund-raising. Franklin rewrote the bill so that the Pennsylvania Assembly would match every private donation up to two thousand pounds.

In both of the compromises he sponsored—the matched funding for the hospital and the idea of the Senate for the Constitution—Franklin merged the other side's views to make the final product better.

Franklin would coin our national motto, "*E pluribus unum.*" He believed not only in the coalition of states but in the merger of ideas.

"Perfection Is the Enemy of the Good"

At the end of the convention, the statesman Franklin said, "I agree to this constitution with all its faults—can a perfect production be expected? I consent, sir, to this constitution because I expect no better and because I am not sure it is *not* the best."

For Franklin's efforts in persuasion, he was called "the Solon of America." The description is apt because it recalls the Athenian politician whose name is now the synonym for *statesman*.

Six centuries before the birth of Christ, the Greek legislator Solon was asked by a friend, "Did you give Athens their best laws?"

"No," replied Solon, "we gave them the best laws they could receive."

In negotiating, Franklin would follow his friend Voltaire's counsel: "Perfection is the enemy of the good."

PUT A GUY'S BACK TO THE WALL AND HE'LL PUT UP HIS BACK

If you demand everything your way, you put the other side against the wall. Henry Kissinger said, "In negotiation leave the other side some back exit, to save face."

Put a guy's back to the wall, and he'll put up his back!

During the time of Franklin, a Colonial militia general called on an Indian chief to negotiate. The chief invited the soldier to sit on the log beside him. When he did, the chief asked him to move farther down. After the officer moved, the chief signaled him to slide farther down, and the officer again repositioned himself.

Then the chief gestured for him to move even farther, and the general said, "But there is no more room—I'll fall off the log."

And the chief replied, "That's what you've done to us—you've pushed us to the sea with your treaties. We can go no farther and we have to fight."

DON'T CONCEDE CONVICTIONS FOR CONSENSUS

In giving way, don't give away the store. That's what was done in Munich and Yalta.

Don't sell out convictions just for consensus.

Don't trade away principles for the peace of appeasement.

At the convention, Franklin agreed to a Senate but not to an unelected, appointed Senate.

In Paris Franklin wouldn't settle just for England ending the war. Britain had to formally recognize the United States of America.

But Franklin could bargain away little provisions to get agreement on big principles.

At the Treaty of Paris conference, Franklin went against the advice of John Adams and included in the American demands a list of reparations to be paid by the British for damage to property. Adams and others thought such demands might make the English walk out.

Franklin—partly because he thought that such reparations might sour Britain's dealings with the new country after the war—dropped the matter in return for formal recognition.

Months later both sides fully reached agreement on the treaty. Then at the last moment, the English balked at signing, saying they would have to go back to London for final approval.

At this point Franklin pulled from his pocket a long list of itemized property damages in pounds to public buildings, churches, and private houses. The British diplomats were so startled that they signed the treaty as it was.

In negotiation and persuasion, concede minor points to conserve major principles.

FIRM ON PRINCIPLES, FLEXIBLE ON PROCEDURE

In 1823 Secretary of State John Quincy Adams tried to persuade President James Monroe to issue a manifesto to Europe warning against interference in the emerging South American nations.

But the secretary of state found his president hesitant. Monroe, the "Era of Good Feelings" president, feared a possible conflict that could lead to war.

Adams appealed to Monroe's pride as the last of the Virginia dynasty of Washington, Jefferson and Madison. Adams said that each had a document of his own to carve his special niche in history—the Farewell Address by Washington, the Declaration of Independence by Jefferson and the Constitution, to a great extent, by Madison. Monroe still wavered.

Then Adams showed Monroe how he could have his cake and eat it too. The manifesto would not be dispatched to envoys, but included in the annual message sent to Congress. It would not even be featured as the subject of the address. Three provisions would be inserted nonconsecutively and sandwiched in between other topics—such as tariffs, postage stamps and harbors—in the fifty-two-item address. The provisions that became known as the Monroe Doctrine were not to be advertised as such.

The result of a "whispered warning," the historic Monroe Doctrine assured Monroe's name in history and it secured Adams's position as successor to Monroe.

By giving way on procedure, Adams established America's first and most famous foreign-policy principle.

IF YOU WANT TO PERSUADE, BE POLITE

A merger lawyer once bluntly spelled out his policy to me on buy outs and takeovers: "Humes, I'll give away perks but grab the power."

Franklin would have accepted that axiom but not the attitude. He once said that in negotiating, "civility is the important thing—not ceremony."

It doesn't cost you a dime as a negotiator to be kind. You don't pay a thing by being polite. You don't lose a thing by listening to everything the other person has to say. And remember, no one ever lost an arm or a leg by lending an ear.

If you mean to convince, be courteous.

If you want to persuade, be polite.

When you want it to go *your way*, give the other side *leeway*.

The rules of persuasion are this: Insist on everything and you'll wind up with nothing. *To be stubborn is sometimes stupid!*

13

Pride and Persuasion
The Perpendicular Pronoun

Once I heard General Eisenhower reminisce about Douglas MacArthur. Eisenhower had served as aide to the general in the Philippines in the late 1930s. Eisenhower said, "You know, MacArthur had an 'eye' problem." I immediately thought that MacArthur had been affected with something like glaucoma or a detached retina. Then Eisenhower added, "MacArthur had a fatal addiction to the perpendicular pronoun—*I*."

Too many are blinded by their own egos when they're trying to influence others. Earlier I told you that Franklin wrote twelve principles of conduct—including the one on integrity, or sincerity. I was wrong and so was Franklin. Franklin did copy down twelve and gave them to an old Quaker friend who told him, "Ben, thou hast forgotten the most important—*humility*." Thus chastised, Franklin added a thirteenth.

THE "I" PROBLEM

Well, maybe you can add some modesty to T-A-L-K-I-N-G. If you can't check your ego, you might as well cross out Timing-Appreciation-Listening-Knowledge-Integrity-Need-Giving.

Think about that. Selfish people are impatient. And impatient people have bad *timing*. They are too quick to seek instant gratification—so they pick the wrong time and place to press their case.

And those who think only of themselves never have any *appreciation* for the other side's angle. They can't seem to see a problem from the other's perspective.

Those who harp only on their own problems never really hear others. Those who talk only on matters that interest them aren't really *listening* to what others have to say. They don't care ... so they don't hear!

And what about the know-it-alls? They're the stupid egotists who don't take the trouble to add to their sum of *knowledge*. They don't bother to learn about another's situation or background.

And then, there is no worse impostor than the person without *integrity*. Those who fool themselves are fakes, and will soon find their proposals as well as their promises given no respect.

As for *need*, if egotists can't admit to themselves their own insecurities, they aren't very likely to be interested in others' needs.

Finally, self-obsessed persons are selfish. Those with gargantuan egos are hardly *giving*: They can't bring themselves to give way even when it could result in their own gain!

Franklin said it when he had Poor Richard say, "A lack of modesty is a lack of good sense."

Check Your Ego at the Door

By the way, "modest" for Franklin wasn't the same as being meek. Franklin didn't become a great statesman by hiding his ideas under a bushel. He had a healthy ego but was no egotist.

The Bible may say, "Blessed are the meek, for they shall inherit the earth," but Franklin knew that the word *meek* is a bad translation of the Greek word *praous*. *Praous* was the word Athenians used to describe a spirited horse that was still ridable. A better translation might be "Happy are those who bridle their own ego, for they shall be big winners."

After the signing of the Constitution, Franklin was the first to greet the crowds outside. An old lady yelled, "Dr. Franklin, did you give us a monarchy or a republic?"

And Franklin answered, "A republic—if you can keep it."

Well, to paraphrase Franklin: *Argument* or *agreement*? *Agreement* if you can keep your ego in check.

Franklin also had Poor Richard say, "Deny self for self's sake!" If all that sounds preachy, it's also practical advice. A little humility is a big part of persuasion.

Franklin didn't mean you had to be a saint to be successful. By the weight of his achievements Franklin might be called a dogooder, but he was no holy roller.

Preachers didn't much like Franklin, and he in turn didn't much like those with a holier-than-thou attitude. In fact, Franklin preferred the sinners. In his autobiography he confessed, "I prefer speckled characters." It reminds one of what Winston Churchill later wrote: "Never trust a man who has not a single redeeming vice."

Stuffed Shirts Don't Sell

Franklin had Poor Richard say, "Wink at small faults—remember thou hast great ones."

But if Franklin had faults, it didn't include the flaunting of his fame and rank. To Franklin, stuffed shirts don't sell—and so in dealing he liked to "dress down."

At a hotel I once saw a chairman of the board blow his stack when his car didn't arrive right on time for a stockholder's meeting. What message did he send to his staff, when he seemed more worried about his limo than the bottom line?

It's one thing for a boss to lose his cool at the loss of profits, but it's another when he blows up at a possible loss of perks. Who likes their boss to act like a brat?

Remember—staffs measure the boss's priorities and go the extra mile accordingly.

I once saw a C.E.O. have his staff mount a full-court press for three weeks arranging for his own private horse carriage to be made available for Prince Philip in Williamsburg—just so he'd get an invite to a White House dinner for the queen.

A lobbyist described a senator to me: "Jamie, when he flies back home, he always has to buy two seats—one for himself and another for his ego."

Compare that with Franklin! One reason he was so successful in persuading other convention delegates is that they all knew he had turned down the chance to be president of the Constitutional Convention and had nominated George Washington instead.

Tommy Lasorda is considered one of baseball's most successful managers. One of his admiring L. A. Dodgers explained the reason: "Tommy is everyone's cheerleader—he persuades you to play your very best *all* the time."

Since 1967 Lasorda has always had the number 2 on his uniform. This year, an outfielder who also wore the number 2 came to the Dodgers in a trade. Tommy offered to give up his number to the new player. But the outfielder, after talking to his wife, said he was so moved by Tommy's generosity of spirit that he chose instead the number 22.

It is hard to imagine a greater contrast to Tommy Lasorda than George Washington! The sight of Lasorda waddling out of the dugout to give out the lineup is hardly the same as the stately stride of General Washington as he assumed the presiding chair at the Philadelphia Convention. But each man showed that persuading his men means putting them first.

Washington inspired a fierce devotion from his men. They knew he could have left his troops at Valley Forge that severe winter of 1777 for a cozier December at Mount Vernon or even at nearby Lancaster.

At a state dinner during the Paris Peace Conference in 1783, Benjamin Franklin watched the French prime minister raise his glass in toast. "To King Louis XVI, the Sun," he said, "in whose radiance the world flourishes." Then he saw the British ambassador stand and say, "To King George III, the Moon, in whose reflection the world glows." Then Benjamin Franklin offered his glass to "General George Washington, the Joshua, who as the Bible says made the sun and moon stop in their appointed tracks."

Franklin respected Washington as one whose devotion to duty persuaded his Continental Army to be no less dedicated.

After the war, when his officers implored him to be king, General Washington rejected the crown. That's command of ego!

Americans pressed General Washington after the convention to become the first president, in part because he never expressed any wish or showed any eagerness for the job.

Washington was elected by acclamation and then would refuse a third term in 1796.

Did Lincoln have an ego problem? When someone saw him shining his own shoes in his White House office, he asked, "Mr. President, why are *you* blacking your own shoes?" And Lincoln responded, "Whose shoes would you have me black?"

MODESTY IS THE MESSAGE

Whether it's shining your own shoes or dialing your own calls, a mark of modesty can send the right message.

General Eisenhower taught me the example of the leader who is so secure that he doesn't have to bolster his ego. A business magnate came to Gettysburg in 1968 after Ike had left the presidency. The industrialist, in talking about the press in the Vietnam conflict, offered this quotation: "Herodotus said in the Peloponnesian Wars that 'you can't be an armchair general twenty miles from the front.' "

I was impressed by the quote and afterward asked Eisenhower, "What were those words of Herodotus?"

Eisenhower smiled and softly answered, "First, it wasn't Herodotus, but Aemilius Paulus. Second, it wasn't the Peloponnesian but the Punic Wars and third, he misquoted." When my surprise at this supposedly nonintellectual general registered on my face, he added, "You don't understand. I got where I did by hiding my ego."

Here was a former president who had no further rungs to climb—yet he saw no reason to flaunt his knowledge. He knew the answer, so why prove how smart he was and embarrass his guest? If you want to persuade, don't parade and pamper your ego.

If you demand attention, you'll have an unwilling audience. When it's others you want to convince, don't act like a princess or a prince! The selfish are not sensitive.

Yet tell me if you know anybody who doesn't describe himself or herself as "sensitive"!

Just take a look at the personals in the back of such city magazines as *New York, Philadelphia* or *The Washingtonian*:

"Good-looking, well-traveled, sensitive, caring professional in middle forties I.S.O. young, slender blonde for meaningful relationship."

"Handsome, fit, young fifty, owner of business, sensitive and caring I.S.O. beautiful woman 25–35 to share boat and life."

Franklin, as a shrewd businessman, just might have printed those personals in his *Almanack*. But he would have repeated Poor Richard's rule, "A lack of modesty is a lack of sense."

Does such conceit suggest someone you'd really find compassionate?

Does such hype hint of any humility?

When I hear people describe themselves as "sensitive" I think of a woman who told the prep-school headmaster, "You don't understand my Kevin. Why, he's such a sensitive child." (Actually, the brat was being given the boot for setting fire to a teacher's cat.)

Do you know why many think they truly are sensitive? Because they think *sensitive* means having their feelings easily hurt. That's not being sensitive—that's being self-absorbed!

In a woman's magazine some years ago I said that a sensitive man was a secure man, and that a true test is just the opposite of almost crying over some imagined slight—it's being able to laugh at himself and his mistakes.

HUMOR AND HUMILITY

The key to humility is humor—a sense of humor about oneself. Take your work seriously, but not yourself! Lighten up and you're more likely to persuade.

General Eisenhower was reviewing troops on a rainy day in England before D-Day. Right in front of a thousand soldiers, he slipped in a mud puddle and fell flat on his fanny. The dead silence of the soldiers was broken as Ike got up and let out a guffaw—and the troops joined in.

Those who laugh at themselves know how to lead others.

After Abraham Lincoln was nominated, a letter came to Springfield from an Eastern magazine requesting that a full biographical background of the presidential candidate be forwarded.

Lincoln wrote back, "A line from the poet would tell it all: 'The short and simple annals of the poor.' "[1]

Compare that to C.E.O.'s who pad their pages in *Who's Who* or make their C.V. a magnum opus.

HIDE CONCEIT AND HAND OUT CREDIT

When you're selling, don't let your ego show. When you're persuading, give the glory to the other guy.

When Nathan Pusey turned over the presidency of Harvard to James Conant, he told him, "You can either do a good job or get the credit for doing a good job but you can't do both!"

Those who succeed assign credit, admit their faults and even their fears.

In April 1945, when Allied troops were poised to cross the Rhine, a jittery GI was edgily pacing in that misty hour

---

[1] Gray's "Elegy Written in a Country Churchyard."

before daylight. A voice called out to him, "Feeling nervous, soldier?"

The private nodded, trying to make out the dim shape coming toward him.

"So am I," responded the advancing figure as he took the younger man by the arm. "Let's both walk along the river together and draw strength from each other."

The GI didn't find out until later that his Rhine companion was the Supreme Allied Commander, General Eisenhower.

Montaigne said, "The valorous admit their vulnerability." To put it another way—only the secure can admit their insecurities.

Benjamin Franklin's autobiography is full of humor directed at himself. His life was not one unbroken pattern of success. He had his share of trials and tragedies. A son, Peter Folger Franklin, had died. William, his first son, whom he fathered out of wedlock, would defy him and take the side of the British in the war.

And Franklin would live to regret his years away from his patient wife in a failing cause to persuade a stubborn Parliament.

Franklin had a long life that spanned every American great from Cotton Mather to James Madison. As a boy he was an assistant to Cotton Mather, the eminent Puritan cleric. Seven decades later James Madison would assist him at the Constitutional Convention.

When Franklin was helping Cotton Mather, he bumped his head as he went to the cellar for an errand. Mather told him, "Ben, you're going to have a lot of bumps in life—shake them off and keep on going."

And it's fitting that Franklin—who first discovered that wearing light clothes in the summer would reflect the heat of the midday sun—would know how to bounce back from calamity and criticism. A self-made man, he understood that the secret of success was subduing the self.

YOU DON'T CONVINCE BY CONTRADICTING

When Thomas Jefferson arrived in Le Havre in 1778 to be minister to France, Count Vergennes said, "Have you come to replace Dr. Franklin?" Jefferson replied, "I have come to succeed Dr. Franklin. No one could ever replace him." Jefferson was once asked what was the secret of Franklin's diplomacy, and he answered, "I never heard of any case when Franklin directly contradicted another."

That's true, because Franklin had a rule: He never introduced his opinions by saying, "Well, it's obvious ..." or "Anyone should know ..." "We all can see ..." or even the words *certainly* or *undoubtedly*.

Franklin wrote in his autobiography that he never "contradicted" but instead would say, "You may be right in some cases, but in this situation it seems to me that ..."

Franklin knew that persuasion is not proving the other guy wrong but rather moving him gently your way.

PERCEIVE AND PERSUADE

Franklin was a Mason. In Paris he attended Masonic meetings with his friend Voltaire. At the Philadelphia lodge, he would see George Washington, who also was a devoted Mason. A central figure in the Masonic rite is King Solomon, who built the temple. The story of the boy Solomon is told in the Bible. An angel visits him and asks, "What do you need to lead your country? Riches? Power? Brilliance of mind?"

And Solomon answered: "Give me an understanding heart."

To understand is to command. And to perceive is to persuade.

Epilogue
New Day

To be a persuader you don't have to be blessed with looks, education or background. Ben Franklin proved that!

Study is the secret—the study of human nature. You have to stop, look and listen.

If you want to persuade one to one, watch the other's eyes, mark the other's words and note the other's language of body and expression.

Perception is the secret of persuasion. To sense another's thoughts is to sell your ideas.

The language of persuasion does not assure power. It does not guarantee results but it does guarantee respect.

It doesn't so much promise success as it does satisfaction—the satisfaction that you have made the most of your God-given skills to advance your own hopes and dreams.

At the close of the Constitutional Convention, Benjamin Franklin offered the motion that all delegates sign the document to affirm their allegiance.

The other delegates approved and then asked Franklin to be the first.

The old statesman, too feeble to walk unaided, made his way to the front table by using the benches to propel himself.

There, he pointed to the chair behind the table, at which Washington often presided. The chair featured the design of a sun low on the horizon.

Franklin then said, "I have often looked at the chair during the vicissitudes of the past session without being able to tell whether it was a rising or setting sun.

"But now I have the satisfaction of knowing it is a rising sun—a new day for America."

And when you sign on to the principles of persuasion by Franklin, you can have the satisfaction of forging new and brighter relationships in office, family and life.

Postscript

In 1790 a dying Benjamin Franklin lay on his bed in his house on High Street, attended by his daughter, Sally. The morning mail brought a letter from the President's House.

Sallie opened the letter for her almost completely blind father. She read aloud President Washington's words:

"If to be venerated for benevolence, if to be admired for talents, if to be esteemed for patriotism, if to be beloved for philanthropy, can gratify the human mind, you have the pleasing consolation to know that you have not lived in vain."

Index

A Note About the Author

Like Benjamin Franklin, James Humes moved to Philadelphia as a young man and has served as both a Pennsylvania legislator and a U.S. diplomat. In 1987, at the request of the U.S. Constitutional Bicentennial Commission, he wrote the one-man show "What's Happening at the Convention, Dr. Franklin?" He also teaches at the University of Pennsylvania, the institution Franklin established. James Humes divides his time between his home in Philadelphia and a Washington, D.C., law office.